The Executive's Compass

James O'Toole

THE EXECUTIVE'S
COMPASS

Business and the Good Society

New York • Oxford • Oxford University Press

Oxford University Press

Oxford   New York
Athens   Auckland   Bangkok   Bombay
Calcutta   Cape Town   Dar es Salaam   Delhi
Florence   Hong Kong   Istanbul   Karachi
Kuala Lumpur   Madras   Madrid   Melbourne
Mexico City   Nairobi   Paris   Singapore
Taipei   Tokyo   Toronto

and associated companies in
Berlin Ibadan

First published in 1993 by Oxford University Press, Inc.,
198 Madison Avenue, New York, New York 10016-4314

First issued as an Oxford University Press paperback, 1995

Oxford is a registered trademark of Oxford University Press

Library of Congress Cataloging-in-Publication Data
O'Toole, James.
The executive's compass : business and the good society
: / James O'Toole.
p. cm.   Includes bibliographical references and index.
ISBN 0–19–508119–6
ISBN 0–19–509644–4 (pbk.)
1. Leadership. 2. Management—Philosophy. 3. Democracy.
4. Corporate culture. I. Title.
HD57.7.O86 1993
658.4—dc20   92–32157

10 9 8 7 6
Printed in the United States of America

For Charles Van Doren
il miglior fabbro

Contents

Foreword

Before I attended the Aspen Institute's Executive Seminar, I was, frankly, skeptical that immersion in the Great Ideas would be of immediate value to me in dealing with the challenges facing a large international corporation. I was soon to learn otherwise.

As Professor James O'Toole points out in this readable and insightful little book, developed during his years of moderating the Aspen seminar, some of the greatest thinkers in history have had much to say about issues that are relevant to contemporary business executives. Aristotle actually conceived of something quite like the futures market, Kant provided a philosophical justification for free market economics, and Locke's theory of property explains why "unearned" capital gains are, in fact, earned as legitimately as salaries and wages.

But learning these things wasn't what surprised me about my Aspen experience. After all, in 1949, when Walter Paepcke, the CEO of the Container Corporation of America, founded the Aspen Institute, he said that the aim was not to sharpen business techniques as such; the Executive Seminar was definitely not intended to make a corporate treasurer a more skilled treasurer.

What surprised me about the seminar was that it did so well what it was intended to do: it made me think. Paepcke said the seminar was designed to help business leaders gain access to their own humanity by making them more self-aware, more self-correcting, and more self-fulfilling. That, I would say, is what it did for me. It helped me focus on those central aspects of corporate leadership that go beyond technical skill and the kind of narrowing preparation one gets in business school. The seminar helps executives to better carry out their responsibilities by deepening their awareness of the roots of their social and political values—and, equally important, the roots of the values of others.

Readers will find that Jim O'Toole captures the essence of that experience in these pages. While that would be a marvelous contribution in itself, he goes further. He provides business leaders with a practical "compass" to help them navigate the turbulent waters of social change and political conflict. With brilliant simplicity, O'Toole's device helps managers identify the ideological origins of contemporary political disagreements and understand the philosophical and ethical sources of our differences of opinion about such issues as executive compensation, plant closings, and environmental regulations.

Once you become familiar with O'Toole's "value compass," you will find yourself saying, "Aha! Now I see why we disagree." The beauty of the compass is that it provides a framework for the executive to create order out of the growing chaos of cultural diversity and conflict of values. Like a real compass, it helps us find where we are, where others are, where we want to go, and how to get there. Like the Aspen experience itself, O'Toole's compass is aimed at developing executive judgment by expanding our understanding of the interrelationship of fundamental values. To managers struggling with strategic global issues of international competition and cooperation, such a "grounding" is of obvious practical use.

Readers will quickly grasp why the comments of Aristotle, Plato, and other ancients about society's problems 2,500 years ago still have practical value. In guiding us through the Aspen seminar readings, O'Toole explains with admirable command of political theory how the democratic process developed during the Enlightenment, and how the views of the writers of that time—Locke, Hobbes, Rousseau, Jefferson, Hamilton, Madison—agree or conflict with Japanese corporatist executives, European Greens, American supply-siders, and "politically correct" egalitarians.

Professor O'Toole makes one thing perfectly clear: Don't go to Aspen—or read his book—looking for agreement. Reasonable people disagree, always have, always will. It is for that reason, O'Toole notes, that the noted philosopher Mortimer J. Adler intentionally built conflict into the selection of readings he assembled for the first Aspen seminar in 1950, the core of which are still read and discussed today.

Over the years, Adler, O'Toole, and the other seminar moderators have found that disagreement can be upsetting to the business mind's preoccupation with order and predictability. But today we are constantly rediscovering that democracy is a lot of things, all of them messy. On the one hand, it seems to lead to gridlock; on the other, to the chaos of special interest politics. But what is this mess, asks O'Toole, if not simply the latest chapter in the 2,500-year-old quest for the good society? He's right, of course, and the best we can hope for is countless more messy episodes to come.

In any case, that's the environment in which we corporate executives must function. Sometimes I catch myself thinking that investing in the oil business in the current risky environment is challenge enough. But today's corporate leader can't simply mind the store; instead, we've got to join wholeheartedly in the task Teddy Roosevelt defined 80 years ago: helping to manage the community, helping to carry the "general load."

Trouble is, as consciousness of individual and group rights continues to develop, judgments about the role of the corporation in society become more difficult and uncertain. From this perspective, ARCO's constituency is as broad as the community itself, and as argumentative. The claims of these stakeholders come to rest, as they should, on my desk.

The poor, the old, those who support our industry on economic grounds, and those who fight us on environmental grounds—all must be dealt with as fairly as possible. But painful tradeoffs are inevitable: investment brings both jobs and pollution; steps to make the corporation more competitive globally lead to unemployment; one person's meat, as always, is another's poison.

Given that reality, it's clear that if business leaders need anything these days, they need a balanced understanding of why the contending forces of democratic societies disagree with one another; they need help in finding their way to wise judgments and good choices; they need, in short, what they will find in this book.

A word of caution: You will *not* find in these pages specific resolutions of the tough value judgments business managers are routinely called on to make—nor did I find such answers at Aspen. What you will find is clarifying evidence that every important issue a business leader faces involves some aspect of the four Great Ideas O'Toole explores: liberty, equality, efficiency, community.

These are obviously Great Ideas that lie at the root of our civilization, and yet every one, as O'Toole points out, is in basic conflict with the other. That's why we can never come to total agreement on a tough, multifaceted issue like, say, the environment. While we grope for environmental policies that will be as fair as possible to these differing values, it is somehow comforting to learn that we're not the first to be challenged by conflicting goals. Wise heads have been working the problem for millenia—and they've had problems, too! The only thing we're sure of is that none of the four primary values—libery, equality, efficiency, community—can safely be sought to the exclusion of the others.

Under those conditions, is any progress possible? O'Toole reminds us that intellectual freedom thrives when every view and opinion is examined without limit or prejudice. He guides us expertly through the currents of thought explored at Aspen, ideas that are strongly but not exclusively in the Western tradition. As the bibliography indicates, the readings include works by men and women, contemporary as well as classical, from Eastern and Western cultures. O'Toole distills their wisdom in a way businesspeople will find fascinating.

In summary, readers will find that Jim O'Toole captures the excitement of the Aspen Executive Seminar in these pages. For that reason alone, the book deserves your attention, particularly if you're a business leader. You and I have much to learn here. But, as Mortimer Adler points out, "solitary reading is as much a vice as solitary drinking." The fullness of the Great Books is made most evident by discussing the ideas. That's why Adler joined the readings with the seminar method. All this will be obvious when you are in Aspen, reading and discussing the Great Ideas with your business colleagues. But even if you don't make it to Aspen, you owe it to youself to look at the seminar's ideas because they are of central concern to all business managers. To begin the process, simply turn the page.

Lodwrick M. Cook
Chairman and Chief Executive Officer
Atlantic Richfield Company

Chapter *1*

Introduction: "Whose Values?"

The central leadership question of the era was posed in two blunt words on a recent cover of *Newsweek*. In bold letters the reader was asked: "Whose Values?"

An answer to that pertinent question was not to be found in the pages of the magazine. The cover story did provide, though, an instructive account of the painful struggles of elected officials endeavoring to choose, among many competing concepts of family values, sexual morality, and social justice, which they should advocate and defend.

Politicians are not alone in having to make such potentially explosive decisions. Business leaders find themselves caught in the same era-defining quandary when they attempt to formulate corporate policy on such contentious issues as plant closings, executive compensation, and affirmative action. Even yesterday's straightforward business questions are, today, fraught with ambiguous moral overtones, and consequent risk for those who must make them. I refer not just to the train of workaday decisions that, willy-nilly, can lead to a tragedy like Bhopal, or the garden-variety financial maneuvers that have been redefined lately as white-collar crimes. Such extreme examples are dramatic but, fortunately, rare.

Almost all managers are now confronted by a mind-boggling complex of social and political issues, the likes of which they have never faced before—even when undertaking routine activities. For instance, establishing a unified corporate policy for coordinating and controlling operations spread across the world has become a sensitive exercise in "cross-cultural empowerment." With the number of layers in the corporate hierarchy greatly reduced, and the complex questions once reserved for senior management now driven further down the organization, few managers remain so apart from the turbulent modern world that they do not have to make choices in the midst of revolutionary change, or try to understand the differing ethical perspectives of those affected. Yet, to turn Milton Friedman's famous phrase on its head, today's managers paradoxically are less "free to choose" than ever before, because the sensitivities of the corporation's many vocal constituencies greatly constrain their range of choice.

Both elected officials and corporate executives are discovering that their institutional systems of response were designed for simpler eras, when the relevant theater of operation was the local community and not the greater world, cross-continental communication took weeks, not split seconds, and society had a predictable, hierarchical order, not the chaotic diversity of mass democracy. Neither public bureaucratic agencies nor private pyramidal organizations were created to cope with the welter of contemporary problems that are global in nature: issues of the environment, international cooperation and competition, and cultural diversity and conflict.

Today's problems, played out on a larger scale than yesterday's, are also complexly interrelated, and thus build demonically on each other. The challenge of coping with these problems is compounded by two paradoxical trends: an implosion of the speed of global communication, and a simultaneous centrifugal explosion of information. These trends conspire to make managers increasingly interdependent while affording them the data to make more independent decisions. As if that weren't recipe enough for conflict and confusion, today we all feel entitled to a say in dealing with the problems that affect us all. The era of the dictator, the czar, the general, the pater-familias, even the traditional boss, has passed in Western society. We—all of us—will rule ourselves; yet we find we speak different tongues, desire different ends, and have different basic assumptions about where society, and the corporations we work in, should be heading. The question indeed is, *"Whose values?"*

In order not to get stuck in this quagmire of complexity, business managers pursue an approach that seems sensible: they simplify. They follow as narrow a path as possible, focus on a single goal or objective, maximize a single business or social value and, perhaps, seek to satisfy a single corporate constituency. This approach is perfectly understandable; it is, after all, exactly what most politicians do in similar circumstances. Unfortunately, it does not fit the challenge at hand. A simple, unidimensional way of looking at problems is unlikely to work in a complex, multidimensional world. That is not to say that appropriate simplification is undesirable; in fact, that should be the goal of policy. Before an executive can usefully simplify, though, she must fully understand the complexities involved. As Justice Oliver Wendell Holmes is reputed to have said, "I would not give a fig for the simplicity this side of complexity, but I would give my life for the simplicity on the other side of complexity."

Abraham Lincoln labored hard and long to reach the simplicity on the other side of complexity exemplified by his compact masterpiece, the Gettysburg Address. Gary Wills has recently reminded us that those 272 words were not, as myth had held, a back-of-the-envelope exercise. To get to the simplicity of "government of the people, by the people, for the people"

Lincoln struggled through countless drafts of the speech and drew painstakingly on the deep reservoir of learning and experience he had accumulated during his long legal and political careers. He was able to convey an inspiring vision to the citizenry because he had spent decades coming to understand the complexity of the ideas Jefferson and the Founders had wrestled with in framing the nation. Until that momentous day in Gettysburg, Americans had thought they had understood the Founders' intent; in fact, they had been confused about the greater purposes of the Union and had failed to appreciate fully what had been proposed by Jefferson "fourscore and seven years" earlier.

At the time Lincoln spoke, dissatisfaction with the American system was widespread even among Northern Unionists. But his clarification of the promise of equality inherent in the Declaration of Independence—his enunciation of a simplicity the other side of complexity—gave the nation the understanding it needed to choose the "new birth" he envisioned for it. Thanks to this singularly impressive act of leadership, the nation ultimately achieved greater unity and effectiveness than it had previously enjoyed.

We need not push to the breaking point the analogy between the challenges Lincoln faced a century and a quarter ago and the challenges corporate executives face in the 1990s. Today there is a groundswell of dissatisfaction with corporate performance among the prime business constituencies— shareowners, customers, employees, and host communities, to cite only four relevant groups. At base, the dissatisfying performance of business stems from the prevailing concept of the role of the corporation. This narrow concept, which evolved in the halcyon 1920s, does not help today's managers to cope with the constantly shifting ground of the complex 1990s. Thus, in growing numbers, managers are abandoning the unidimensional premises that have driven their behavior and are changing the tunes their corporations have played for decades. Witness the sudden conversion of Jack Welch, CEO of General Electric. Overnight he went from espousing Connecticut common sense (in which all problems are reduced to three sentences, the first of which is, "It's really quite simple") to Lincolnesque corporate statesmanship; he now acknowledges the complexity of the problems GE faces and concedes that he cannot solve them all himself.

Like Welch, numerous corporate managers now seek a more comprehensive and sophisticated concept of what they do and why, a concept that will also give them a useful framework for choosing what to do and how to do it. They have seen that in simply stressing one value (individual competition, for example), they sacrifice other equally necessary values (such as cooperation). Experience in the hard-knocks school of the 1980s has taught them that the art of leadership requires the simultaneous pursuit of several values—values that, in the simplicity *this* side of complexity, appear incompatible.

The simplicity the *other* side of complexity offers a different prospect: that incompatible values might be made mutually achievable and reinforcing. The leadership challenge, then, is to get to the other side of complexity. But how does one get there? Only one sure route has been identified: the enhancement of understanding. To move beyond the confusion of complexity, executives must abandon their constant search for the immediately practical and, paradoxically, seek to understand the underlying ideas and values that have shaped the world they work in.

Four decades of experience at The Aspen Institute's celebrated Executive Seminar have shown that executives can gain this understanding by studying of the great ideas of political economy and moral philosophy. Committing themselves to some challenging reading, they arrive at truly useful simplicity, and at effective, practical applications of it. For men and women whose most common complaint is lack of time and too much to read, the good news is that the time invested in such

study is time spent in preparing to apply enhanced understanding to managerial tasks—an understanding that, furthermore, differentiates management from leadership. For example, alumni of the Aspen Executive Seminar report that they've
gained an increased awareness of the sources of both conflict
and consensus in society, and thus are better prepared to navigate their institutions' passage through the increasingly turbulent seas of social, political, and economic change. That's the
stuff of leadership. Further, unless executives do understand
the sources of these conflicting views of the good society, they
will be condemned to see the process of democracy as a blur.
Worse, those who are incapable of seeing the process clearly
are incapable of responding appropriately to the threats and
opportunities presented by social change.

Realistically, a full understanding of the great ideas of
political economy requires a lifetime of reading, thought, and
discussion. Even the two-week Aspen Executive Seminar (the
readings for which constitute the bibliographic core of this
book) can do little more than illustrate the benefits of a broad
vision informed by deepened understanding, and the two
hours it takes to read this book offer only a glimmer of the
practical potential of that vision. This is only an executive
summary, designed to entice the reader into further consideration of the ideas that have gone into the making of today's
world. The small, related set of ideas it focuses on, though, are
of such overriding significance that they readily serve as a
springboard to understanding many other contemporary issues
in business and society. One caveat: the function of a springboard is to propel one out into deep water; the reader must be
wary of the comforting belief that treading through this brief
digest will provide the same depth of insight as swimming in
the original texts!

The following pages offer brief, nontechnical introduc-
tions to what some of the finest minds of Western civilization
have had to say about the essential elements of the good society

(with attention, where relevant, to parallels and differences in non-Western philosophy). We then explore the ways Americans in the 1990s think about the same issues and ideas that have engaged the minds of men and women for centuries. In so doing, we examine the ideologies, or systems of belief, we use—often unconsciously—to make sense out of the philosophical muddle.

As a guide to this vast historical and intellectual territory, we will make use of a "compass card," a quadrant on which the polar positions are the ideas of liberty, equality, efficiency, and community:

Liberty

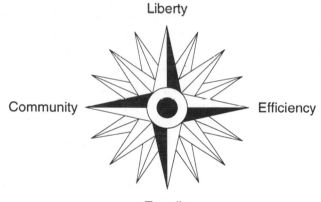

Community — Efficiency

Equality

The tensions among these four ideas create what historian James MacGregor Burns calls "the deadlock of democracy."

Our goal is to get past executives' often-voiced frustration with this deadlock to an appreciation of the necessity of tension in the process of democratic change. First we will examine why these four great ideas are the major elements out of which a well-functioning democracy might construct "the good society"; we then explore the implications for corporations, and end with practical applications of what we have learned.

We will use this quadrant as a tool to help us draw useful connections between the past and present, and between the

philosophical and the practical. Since the logic and applications of the compass card are not self-evident, this book can be
seen as a user's guide to this practical device, whose function is
to help executives get to the simplicity the other side of complexity.

The ideas discussed in these pages are the grist of what
Mortimer Adler calls "the great conversation across the centuries." Executives engaged in contemporary debates about the
taxation of capital gains, regulation of auto emissions, national
health insurance, and affirmative action are participants in that
same great conversation, which has been ongoing for over two
thousand years—whether they realize it or not. For that matter,
they are a part of it whether they wish to be or not, because the
citizenry increasingly believe that the relationship between
business and government is a key to the making of the good
society. In the eyes of most Americans, executives play an equal
or greater role than politicians in that endeavor.

This review is intended to be useful to executives in five
roles they play: One, as managers engaged in making "purely
business" decisions: by recognizing and properly addressing
the broad social implications of such decisions, they can bring
out more effective organizational performance. Two, as managers whose internal policies turn out to affect outside constituencies. Three, as managers who are participants and partners
in government (that is, executives themselves are political
players when they act as contractors, campaign contributors,
and subjects of laws in whose making they have had a voice).
Four, as citizens who vote and volunteer in the political process. Finally, five, as individuals who choose to examine their
own lives and their own potential legacies to society.

The achievement of our stated goal of enhanced understanding is impeded by familiarity. The key words we use in
this enquiry are part of the working vocabulary of every literate
citizen, and executives may have trouble seeing the practical
value of reexamining what they believe they've understood

since their school days. As my Aspen Institute colleague Charles Van Doren explains, our subject is "something that executives think they already know. But the record of forty years of Aspen Executive Seminars demonstrates that they don't. The subject is on the tip of their tongues at all times, but their understanding of it is shallow and in many respects incorrect." In effect, because we all use the words liberty, equality, efficiency, community, and democracy in our professional lives, we too readily assume we understand the concepts behind those words and, further, assume that we understand the relationships among them.

As Van Doren notes, experience indicates that this assumption is often unfounded. And when wisdom is a false premise, it presents a danger to those who embrace it. What we mistakenly assume we know can hurt us, as executives painfully discover when they scramble without sufficient depth of knowledge to cope with such complex issues as plant closings, layoff policies, executive compensation, consumerism, environmentalism, PACs, minority hiring, relations with institutional investors, "unfair" foreign competition, multiculturalism, inner city investment, employment practices that affect family life, and so on. The almost daily complaints reported in the business press about the dearth of corporate leadership testify to the fact that executives deal with such value-based issues no more effectively than elected officials deal with their own similarly complex agendas. Since almost all managers ultimately are forced to deal with these leadership issues, the question comes down to whether they will deal with them well or badly.

These are leadership issues because, in the final analysis, they require moral judgments on the part of decision makers. (Decisions based solely on technical knowledge require no leadership.) Moral choices made by leaders can be informed only by a deepened understanding of the ideas that history's greatest political economists and moral philosophers explicated for the benefit of future generations. These ideas constitute a part of the inherited legacy of civilization that we are all entitled to exploit. Indeed, it is foolhardy in the extreme to fail to draw upon this rich source of knowledge.

Executives' continued failure to understand (thus to deal effectively with) the complex problems listed above would be extremely costly. Hence this is a special kind of how-to book, the mastery of which has bottom-line implications; yet, it should not be confused with the brand of how-to books replete with formulaic advice—simplicity this side of complexity. A manager will not learn in these pages how to handle the current hassle over this or that question of regulatory compliance which happens to be on her desk. Such questions are either straightforward technical matters (requiring lawyers, not leaders, to explicate), or are unique in nature, thus, requiring the exercise of moral judgment. The latter questions require managerial leadership, and no how-to book can remove that burden from the shoulders of the executive. As Peter Drucker writes, the task and responsibility of management is to choose between ambiguous courses of action.

The ideas presented in these pages are *useful*, though, in learning that art: leadership. These ideas can help executives to understand the moral and philosophical essence of the problems they face, and once they understand those problems' underlying complexity, their options for action clarify. One's felt need for nuts-and-bolts advice and practical formulae recedes when one gains understanding of underlying philosophical concepts. Managers who clamor for how-to instruction are, by definition, stuck on the near side of complexity.

Another purpose of this book is to refocus the discussion of business and society in light of the astonishingly complete collapse of communism. When Mortimer Adler developed the Aspen Executive Seminar in the 1950s, the dominant issue was, and remained, for nearly four decades, the tension between communism and capitalism. That Western democracies faced a clear ideological adversary had, in the words of Aspen's

Joseph Nye, "the effect of polarizing the domestic debate." But now, Nye predicts, "A whole complex of issues regarding how we think of ourselves, which was locked up in the world of bipolar competition, is going to become unstuck." The great ideas discussed here can be as useful a guide to this new world as they were to the old—since we face not the end of history, in which all the problems of political economy are resolved, but the beginning of an era, in which we are free to explore alternative solutions to the intransigent problems facing capitalist democracies. We can engage now in the "great conversation" without the distraction of arguing with the ideological friends, or enemies, of Karl Marx.

Robert Heilbroner has warned, "Just because socialism has lost does not mean that capitalism has won." The burden, and the skeptical eye of millions, is upon America and the West to demonstrate that capitalism can raise standards of living and at the same time respect the dignity of each individual human being. It may be mistaken to assume that democracy now will prevail in the majority of the world's nations, where it has yet to take root. That assumption ignores the fact that the enemies of democracy are dedicated and are legion. Confronted by them, democrats can only win the day if they successfully practice what they preach. Because the case for democracy must be made by example, it is incumbent on those who have benefited from the system to recommit themselves not only to its defense and propagation, but to making it work better in their own homelands. America and the democratic, capitalist West now have a rare historical opportunity to create the good society as a model for the world. Leadership for that effort must come as much from the business community as from those in elected office.

Furthermore, as the globalization of markets and the spread of popular culture by way of telecommunications make the world increasingly homogenized, the ideas explored here are becoming pertinent to non-Western nations adopting Western-style democracies, economies, and technologies. More than ever, then, it is incumbent on people from all nations to understand more fully the increasingly global search for the good society—whose main vehicle, for better or worse, is a business culture rooted in Western concepts. This statement is neither an endorsement of existing business values nor an apology for so-called cultural imperialism. As we shall see, many of the ideas of the West mesh naturally with existing concepts in non-Western cultures, and contact with ideas of other cultures is profitably modifying Western concepts. Our goal here is not indoctrination, but understanding. In these singularly contentious times, we seek to find areas of common ground where we may all learn to live and work together.

The reader is entitled to know my qualifications to serve as guide to this enquiry and a full disclosure of my agenda and political leanings. By education, I am a social anthropologist, someone who seeks to understand the behavior of exotic cultures, and especially his own. By occupation, I am a professor of management, someone who looks for ways to help business leaders be more effective. By inclination, I am a political economist: in that role I have been a moderator in The Aspen Institute's Executive Seminar for some two decades. There I have enjoyed great intellectual rewards as I've struggled along with corporate leaders to make sense of the readings on political economy and political philosophy outlined in these pages. Since I wish everyone could participate in an experience like Aspen, my unhidden agenda includes enticing practical men and women to read and discuss the great books outlined here (for a full listing, see the bibliography). Finally, if my bias is not already manifest, I am an unapologetic believer in democracy. I warn readers that my other intent is to convince them that the cure for the undeniable ills of our maddening democracy is, paradoxically, more democracy.

Chapter *2* ≡

Why We Disagree

Americans tend to disagree about most matters of public concern. In fact, that's putting it mildly. Recent pitched encounters in Washington over proposed reforms of the income tax, social security, welfare, and health care systems, not to mention contentious confirmation battles over Supreme Court nominees, reveal deep fault lines in the nation's ideological substrata. Moreover, when debating such issues, we seem to fire from all directions at once in an incoherent, scattershot pattern of dissonance, discord, and disunity. Consider the testimony presented at recent Congressional hearings on a proposed overhaul of the Clean Air Act: labor leaders, industrialists, environmentalists, big-city mayors, public health officials, and free-market economists, to cite only the most vocal petitioners, each advanced a different position on the proposed new emissions standards. Divergence and disharmony ruled in the Capitol hearing room as these often antagonistic parties engaged in a multisided ideological melee. The overheated hearings became a special interest pressure cooker, and what was left at the end was an unpalatable residue of public policy.

Nearly everyone was dissatisfied with the new standards. Given that such messy conflicts are now televised around the clock, it is hardly surprising that increasing numbers of citizens view democratic government as one or more of the following: unresponsive, ineffective, immobilized, chaotic. In particular, frustrated businesspeople often find the process unfathomable, even anarchic, when it impinges, as it inevitably does, on their special concerns. Their confusion and occasional anger are understandable. When an issue affecting one's livelihood is caught in the maelstrom of representative democracy, it takes heroic objectivity to maintain a positive view of the system. Under such circumstances even the most tolerant souls are likely to see "the mess in Washington" as irrational and unfair. Cynics go a step further, declaring that the only constants in public affairs are the unprincipled pursuits of individual self-interest and group special interest.

The depressing facts critics of modern democracy offer are accurate, but one can take a more positive view of the seeming chaos and see a method to the madness; one can see the disorderly process as the latest development in the noble, albeit uneven, 2,500-year quest for the good society. While the end of that search remains elusive, I am convinced that the search itself is not illusive. Indeed, the purpose of this book is to reveal the underlying intellectual order of that centuries-old quest, so that businesspeople can make better sense of a democratic system that appears ineffective and unresponsive at best and, at worst, careening out of control. I hope that my practical-minded readers will come to see that the good society may be forged only out of such turmoil, and that it is in their interest to understand more fully the maddening process of democratic change.

Admittedly, the good society is an abstract and subjective concept. Typically, such a society is defined in terms of *justice:* the good society is a just society because the essential rights of every citizen are secured. However, even when we use that common, and essentially valid, definition, we have raised more questions than we have answered. What, if anything, is every citizen entitled to receive from society? As we shall see, the very source of the observed gridlock and chaos of democracy results from competition among several differing answers to that question.

When quarreling parties are squared off in deep and abiding disagreement, the prudent mediator attempts to break the deadlock by encouraging the disputants to step back and find an area of fundamental agreement. If that shared belief is basic enough, the parties then might be able to see why they disagree, and come to respectfully agree to disagree. We should aim for nothing less as the end of our enquiry.

Fortunately, there is remarkable consensus on a fundamental point: *The task of every legitimate government is to secure the good society for its citizens.* Nearly every political philosopher from Aristotle to Max Weber has agreed that the provision of a good (or just) society is the end purpose of government. Unfortunately, that rare meeting of minds is not the end of the question; it is where the real problems start. Of all the writers who came along during the two and a half millennia between Aristotle and Weber—that is, the great thinkers whose works are sandwiched in the library between those two alphabet-spanning individuals—*every last one of them defined the good society differently.*

Here's a sampling of how those great minds have defined the good or just society:

- To Aristotle, it permits some of its members to live "the good life."
- To Hobbes, it provides sufficient order to allow material progress.
- To Locke, it guarantees life, liberty and property.
- To Rousseau, it preserves as much as possible of the conditions of liberty and equality that humankind enjoyed in "the state of nature."
- To Adam Smith, it has nearly absolute economic freedom.

- To Thomas Jefferson, it consists of people who live in small-scale, rural communities characterized by a high quality of life.
- To Alexander Hamilton, it consists of people who live in modern industrial cities characterized by a high standard of living.
- To Marx, it has nearly absolute economic equality.
- To J. S. Mill, it allows nearly absolute social freedom.
- To Harriet Taylor Mill, it allows women to enjoy the equality of opportunity with men.
- To Weber, it is governed by laws, so that no citizen is treated arbitrarily.
- To Martin Luther King, it guarantees the "natural rights" of all its members, without regard to their race, sex, religion, or class.

And on and on, with dozens of other authors offering permutations and variations on each of these visions (I have oversimplified each to illustrate the great divergence of opinion on this, the most fundamental of all social questions.)

Cut to the absolute core, almost all political debate and conflict revolves around competing ideas of what constitutes the good or just society. This fact raises several important questions:

Why are the most brilliant minds of history in such stark disagreement over the issue they all agree is the most important?

How do various contemporary individuals and groups define the good society, and why?

Which, if any, of these many views deserves to prevail?

How, with so many competing views, can government be said to provide the good society to all?

What role do modern corporations play in the pursuit of the good society, and what role should they play?

In the pages that follow, the reader will find not answers to these questions but a framework for thinking about them. In the final analysis, we must each make up our own minds about the nature of the society we wish to live in; my purpose is not to make Tories out of Whigs or vice versa. I seek to help each, according to her preferences, become a more thoughtful Tory or a more thoughtful Whig! If in that process of discovery we should each find that the others' views are as legitimate as our own, the prospects of a productive resolution of our national differences might be enhanced. (My last point is not a prelude to an argument for the moral relativism in vogue in academia; as we shall discover, the belief that anything goes—that all value systems are of equal merit—is ethically bankrupt and is the antithesis of the moral symmetry these pages describe.)

Our mode of enquiry will be based on the analysis of dreams. I should say collective dreams, because what we are about has nothing to do with individual psychology, or with psychology at all, for that matter. The dreams we shall analyze are the wide-awake kind. Such dreams are a part of national character, as much manifestations of culture as rituals and rites, taboos and totems. Anthropologists tell us that Australian aborigines dream of the glorious past of their ancestors, the better world that existed before the Europeans arrived in the Antipodes. After World War II, New Guineans were said to dream of the return of American cargo ships laden with the material wealth of the West. Haven't Poles always dreamt of independence? Don't Russian Orthodox Christians (and Islamic fundamentalists) dream of theocracies past and future? And don't some of these dreams actually come true? Witness the German dream of unification. Such collective dreams are almost always concerned with an imagined better world than the one that exists.

Then there are Americans. We dream of economics! After all, as Calvin Coolidge observed, "The business of America is business," and it's no accident that the American Dream is a rags-to-riches climb to the top. While that dream is the baseline, in fact we have many competing dreams, each emanating from a particular view of the good society. One constant that

runs through all these competing American dreams is the
emphasis on the relationship between society and the productive enterprises that turn out goods and services. In short, no
matter what Americans may dream, it boils down for good or ill
to a vision of entrepreneurs and corporations, of the Mom 'n
Pop store and General Motors. Put another way, Americans of
all ideological leanings see the behavior and performance of
productive enterprises as powerfully influencing the extent to
which the public experiences society as good. Consequently,
the central political question is how (or whether) to control,
direct, or tweak business's behavior to produce the good society.

If the good society means different things to different people, though—if we each have our own unique dreams—how in
the devil's name can such diffuse objectives be addressed? If
we all have different dreams (call them values, objectives, ideals, or desires), is there any practical way to please everybody?

No, we can't all be made perfectly happy, because there is
no way in a free society to force or entice all citizens to share the
same ultimate vision. But yes, in another sense everyone can be
satisfied. At a minimum, we can all feel that the system is
legitimate—that is, that we all get a fair hearing. To insure that
fair hearing is the prime function of democracy. For all its
manifest shortcomings, democracy, because it allows a fair
hearing to all ideas, is the only system capable of providing a
sense of legitimacy to a large and complex society. Moreover, I
hope to demonstrate that democratic society at its best can go
much further and institute policies that are responsive to the
many competing claims, without creating a wishy-washy compromise that satisfies no one.

A rather simple theory supports these two admittedly opti-
mistic assertions. Since this theory is based on common sense
and everyday experience, I trust it will appear no more obscure
than the principles of pluralism and democracy on which it is
based. To understand this theory, we must begin with what

George Will calls the four "great themes of political argument." My basic contention is that there are four such themes, or dreams: liberty, equality, efficiency, and community. The countless competing views of the good society propounded over the millennia, and the positions staked out on most issues being debated today in Washington and local governments, can be sorted into these four dreams.

Americans have always resisted examining the philosophical roots of their differences current and past. We have tended to repress these dreams out of fear of the charge of being ideological—anti-American—if we were to let them surface. We much prefer to think of ourselves as a pragmatic nation, even if that means blinding ourselves to the causes of our disagreements and preventing ourselves from arriving at a practical resolution based on an understanding of our true differences.

What if we were to let these dreams surface and acknowledge them? Might not this act of analysis help us to understand ourselves and the sources of conflict in our society better, and to see more clearly the choices we face as a nation? If Sigmund Freud were available (and willing to make a midcareer change and become a political philosopher), we might call on him to put the nation on the couch and interpret its four recurrent dreams: "Now, perhaps, ve shall begin . . ."

≡ Dream One: Liberty

In this reverie we live in a totally free economy where the only law is that of supply and demand. The image of an oriental bazaar comes before the eyes. Anything and everything is for sale, and at no fixed price. There is a dynamism and clatter akin to the action on the floor of the Chicago commodity exchange, but this "pit" is not bounded by the walls of a regulated board of trade. The market is in the streets.

The last such free markets were to be found in places like

Beirut, Tangiers, and Hong Kong in the 1960s, where American visitors discovered hawkers dealing in gold and currency, competing with each other as they dickered with customers over the price of dollars, marks, and rubles (shoeboxes full of the latter available for a song). Like so many British bookies busily chalking up changing odds, the merchants frenetically altered their asking rates through a complex process of competitive haggling. To the visitor, there was more than just the excitement of the hustle; there was a tinge of forbidden fruit, since Americans were not allowed to trade in gold at the time, and one needed a license to deal in currencies, and even then, never in the streets.

In free ports and open cities around the world, almost every form of restraint of trade—taxes, tariffs, regulations, licensing, zoning—has been absent at one time or another. In such places, alleys and avenues become markets attracting a fantastic variety of goods and services. This scene is the world of the entrepreneur, Horatio Alger, innovation, and what Americans rather chauvinistically call Yankee ingenuity.

Significantly, when Americans dream of such places, what entices them is neither greed nor the excitement of the bazaar, but the social and political consequences of the free market. These dreamers, whom we will call Libertarians, believe that a free economy is a prerequisite for a higher-order good: a free polity. To these advocates of rugged individualism, the good society is one with absolute political and economic liberty.

≡ Dream Two: Equality

To others, the dream of free markets is a nightmare. (Disembarking in Beirut in the late 1960s, an American visitor was accosted by an enterprising young Arab boy: "Say, mister, you want to buy gold? No? How about diamonds? Hashish? Some harder drug? Perhaps a lovely woman?" Finally, in desperation for a sale, "You want to buy *me?*") In the rialto, those whom we will call Egalitarians see the losers as well as the winners, the social costs as well as the benefits.

To Egalitarians, thoughts of a free market conjure up visions of the Dickensian slums that historically accompanied unregulated markets, of the "dark satanic" mills of Manchester, England and Lowell, Massachusetts. They recall the historical exploitation of women, children, and minorities, of lives made brutish and short by poverty, disease, and drugs. In short, in unregulated capitalism they see a system with unacceptably large inequalities of income and power. They see disparities not only in standards of living, but in levels of civilization existing side-by-side in the same nation—differences that reflect not legitimate rewards for contribution but the random payout of a system that knows no more of justice than a casino.

Traditionally, American Egalitarians have sought to use the power of government to reduce the great disparities in wealth and opportunity they see around them. When they dream of the good society, visions of Scandinavia dance in their heads. In recent years, many American Egalitarians have become less concerned with inequalities based on social class than with addressing injustices in the treatment of such disempowered groups as women, racial minorities, homosexuals, the aged and the handicapped.

≣ Dream Three: Efficiency

Others see in the dream of the bazaar only a romanticized past. Because the economies of the world are now interdependent, dominated by large corporations, and characterized by complex technologies, those we shall call Corporatists disparage the Libertarian model of "competing lemonade stands" as simplistic and out-of-date. Impressed by the success of the Japanese and Western European political economies, Corporatists dream of creating American parallels to those countries' cooperative arrangements among business, government, and labor.

Corporatists believe that a good society is predicated on full employment and a constantly improving standard of living. They believe in the necessity of wealth creation through the most productive applications of science and technology. Since the achievement of their dream requires economic growth, they would use every means at the disposal of the entire society to motivate large business enterprises to produce at maximum efficiency. To this end, they advocate a national industrial policy designed to encourage the most productive investments in new products and technologies and in human resources.

☰ Dream Four: Community

To our last group, the dream about a Corporatist state is a nightmare—of great belching smokestacks, alienated workers in giant, dehumanizing bureaucracies, and powerless citizens being crushed beneath the combined weight of big business, big government, and big unions. These, the Communitarians, believe that a high quality of life is more important than a high standard of living. They advocate environmentalist policies to conserve natural resources, halt conspicuous consumption, and end pollution. Because they are humanists, they argue that machines should serve people, not vice versa, and that people should be respected as ends, not as resources in industrial processes. They worry that uncontrolled applications of powerful technologies threaten the moral foundations of culture and humanity.

Communitarians feel that decentralization furthers the good society by creating a sense of face-to-face community; they look to traditional family and neighborhood values to lead people to the benefits of cooperation over life-threatening competition. They dream of a borderless world whose numerous communities feel linked to each other by shared responsibilities. In essence, they want all people to feel a part of a worldwide community of humankind, responsible for the future of our tiny planet. Perhaps paradoxically, some American multiculturalist Communitarians have begun to advocate the celebration of the diversity of humankind, with each ethnic group comprising its own unique community.

These four dreams tug like polar forces at the American system of government and at the society as a whole. The extreme adherents of each position have their own mutually incompatible goals or ideals, and their own divergent views as to the proper relationship of business to society. Of course, few Americans are extremists; only a very few are true believers committed one hundred percent to any one of these ideologies. I've presented the extremes for the sake of clarity and to illustrate how these polar positions are in constant conflict with each other:

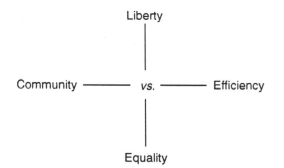

As graphically represented, these four "great themes of political argument" are trade-offs with each other, zero-sum positions in which an increment of one value leads to a consequent, equivalent loss of its opposite. Throughout history, political philosophers have argued that societies face exactly such tragic choices. They would argue that this problem is why, today, America has no national consensus about what constitutes the good society, and why government seems immobilized and ineffective. Here is how Isaiah Berlin states the conventional wisdom on the issue of the inevitable collision of values: "The notion of the perfect whole, the ultimate solution, in which all good things coexist, seems to me to be not merely unattainable—that is a truism—but conceptually incoherent; I do not know what is meant by a harmony of this kind. Some among the Great Goods cannot live together." But are those who think like Berlin correct in coming to this tragic conclusion? Do the facts support the conclusion that society is doomed to irreconcilable conflict? Do our undeniable differences preclude cooperative, concerted, and effective action on the problems facing the nation, or is there some process that can lead to an acceptable resolution of the four apparently conflicting concepts of the good society?

John Gardner describes the challenge in this way: "The play of conflicting interests in a framework of shared purposes is the drama of a free society. It is a robust exercise and a noisy one, not for the faint hearted or the tidy-minded. . . . Wholeness incorporating diversity is the transcendent goal of our time."

Before we begin to think about possible ways of overcoming value conflicts, let us first establish the business credentials of a few of the key figures cited in these pages. (For a brief identification of any of these authors, see the Name Index.) Aristotle, for example, described the workings of a prototypical futures market some four hundred years before the Christian era. This famous tutor of Alexander the Great explained the benefits of the division of labor and economies-of-scale, which Adam Smith supposedly first identified 2,200 years later. Aristotle even forecast the coming of automation, outlining the socioeconomic advantages of what we now call robotics. A few years earlier, Aristotle's teacher, Plato, had propounded a theory of hierarchical organizations, arguing the case for efficient governance by professional managers, anticipating Peter Drucker by two and a half millennia. Before Plato, Sophocles had stolen the thunder from even the redoubtable Tom Peters when he showed that the ability to listen is a key trait of effective leadership!

Jumping ahead to the seventeenth century, John Locke was a hop and a skip ahead of Boone Pickens in articulating a rationale that moderns might use to defend shareholder rights. Between 1800 and 1820, in the world's largest and most profitable factory of the time, industrialist Robert Owen demonstrated the productive potential of what are today called Japanese management practices. Thirty years later, John Stuart Mill outlined to the fineness of a gnat's eyebrow the details of George Bush's 1990s educational initiative, right down to the vouchers. The first person to predict the growth of giant multinational corporations—and to sing their praises—was none other than Karl Marx. As impressive as such business forecasts are, though, the reader will find that the most practical writings of the great minds are addressed, paradoxically, to what are seemingly the most abstract social questions. Making that discovery will be the greatest joy of the journey before us, a 2,500-year voyage of the mind.

As we make that voyage in the four sections that follow, we shall discover the origins of America's social dreams of liberty, equality, efficiency, and community. As we look backward from the present, we will begin to see more clearly what we believe and why, what others believe and why, and where all these various beliefs come from. With that enhanced knowledge, we may then each formulate for ourselves our own informed answers to the question that bedevils modern democracy: Can the good society be created in a world of conflicting values?

Chapter _3_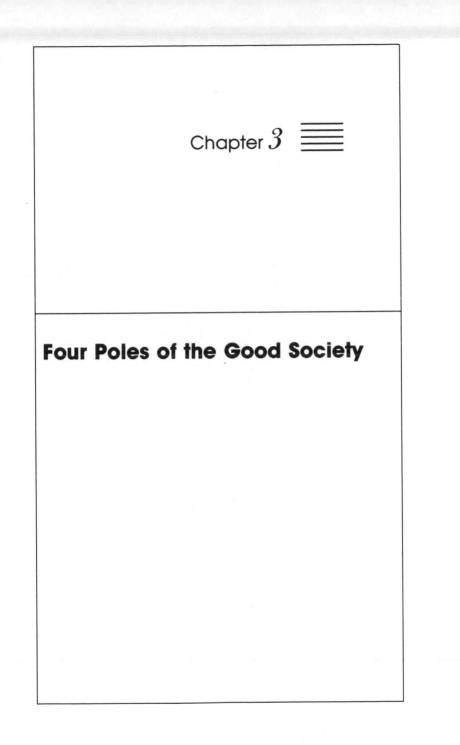

Four Poles of the Good Society

≡ Liberty

Liberty is the brightest star in the firmament of Western social values. As the second millennium of the modern era ends, the West has suddenly reached a near consensus that it is best to rely "on voluntary cooperation and private enterprise," and that such market freedom is a natural complement to freedom of thought, speech, and religion. Moreover, belief in the inherent right to individual liberty appears to be spreading to parts of Asia and the Third World, where the idea of freedom has for the first time become a serious intellectual subcurrent.

For three hundred years liberty has been, and remains today, particularly important in the Anglo-American political tradition. As if to underscore that centrality, the English language contains two perfectly synonymous words that convey the concept of individual independence: the Latinate *liberty* and the Germanic *freedom*. Paradoxically, while these two words are interchangeable, there exist perhaps half a dozen different definitions of the abstract concepts they represent;

more confusing still, they describe action in three distinct spheres: religion, politics, and economics.

Setting aside here the oldest issues in these three realms—religious questions concerning the exercise of free will—we find that the concept of political liberty is of surprisingly recent origin; it came into currency in seventeenth-century England when subjects of the Crown first began to challenge the divine right of kings. The concept of economic freedom was not introduced until over a century later when Adam Smith unveiled the notion of laissez faire in the memorable year 1776.

Political Liberty

While the modern idea of political freedom dates back only three centuries, one can find intimations of the concept in classical literature. In the fourth century B.C., the Athenians danced around the idea of political liberty, as one might expect from a society engaged in the world's first democratic experiment. In *Antigone,* modern readers find that Sophocles raises the issue of the conflict between individual conscience and the laws of the state. A historical reading of this timeless play reveals, however, that Sophocles was not primarily interested in what moderns see as the classic struggle between law and liberty; to the ancients, *Antigone* was a tragedy about a ruler who made a bad decision and had to choose between two equally evil alternatives, and whose fatal flaw was that he could not admit his mistake.

Modern readers are similarly tempted to find a violation of freedom of speech in Plato's account of Socrates being forced to take the hemlock. But Plato was no lover of liberty as we would use that term: to him, the good society is one led by the best and the brightest, "guardians" who insure the "virtue" of the state regardless of the desires of the citizenry. This inequality of political rights is hardly proto-Libertarian. Aristotle, too, comes enticingly close to grasping the modern notion of freedom, but at best he speaks of a kind of freedom for the few. While not quite the critic of democracy his teacher Plato was, Aristotle believed in rule by a small class of "freemen and equals" (in the eyes of almost all the ancients, some were born to rule, others to be ruled). Like Plato, Aristotle's true interest and concern was inequality, and not freedom. The inherent justice of inequality is a major subtheme in modern Libertarian thought, as we shall see; the Greeks, though, did not come close to advocating individual freedom. When it comes to liberty in the modern sense, the Greeks' idea of it amounted to little more than the freedom enjoyed by children on a well-run school playground.

As with so much of our intellectual inheritance, the modern notion of political liberty is a product of the Enlightenment. It was Hobbes who introduced, in *The Leviathan,* the concept that humans are really free only in the "state of nature"—an idea subsequently to take hold as the basis for the call for political rights that would incite a century of rebellion culminating in the American and French revolutions. Ironically, to stir the call for liberty was the opposite of Hobbes's intent; he had set out to write an apologia for the illiberal Stuarts. In the process of making his argument, though, he posited the problematic idea of the state of nature (a condition anthropologists today regard as pure fantasy, and philosophers as a convenient assumption). In nature, man "finds no stop in doing what he has the will, desire or inclination to do." To Hobbes the "Natural Right" of every individual in this Edenic state is "the liberty each man has to use his own power for the preservation of his own nature, that is to say his own life . . . and consequently of doing anything which in his own judgment and reason he shall conceive to be the aptest means thereunto." Here, particularly in the concluding phrase, we see a statement of a modern notion of liberty. But in the next breath Hobbes gives it all away! Unhappily, he says, in this free and natural state the condition of life is "solitary, poor, nasty, brutish and short" because there is a perpetual "war . . . of every man against every man." Hence, to procure security, and the progress of civilization, humans reluctantly surrender the liberty of nature, entering into a "social contract" to live under the rule of law.

In essence, humankind exchanges its natural liberty for the security an all-powerful monarch guarantees. To all the world (with the exception, perhaps, of the monarch and Hobbes) this is a bitter bargain. Little wonder that the world looked with greater favor on the variation the liberal anti-Stuart John Locke sang on the same Natural Rights/social contract theme forty years later. To Locke, mankind in a state of nature "is free from any superior power on earth." That sounds a lot like the first movement of Hobbes's political oratorio, but there is an important difference: Locke's state of nature is relatively benign, marred only by conflicts over property. In his second movement, Locke provides his audience with a harmonious conclusion: the bargain humankind strikes in entering a civil state is no worse than what existed in the state of nature; in fact, it is better. That is so because civil liberty is a state of freedom "under no other legislative power but that established by consent."

To get to this happy state, Locke went back to the forgotten arguments of Hobbes's contemporaries, the Levellers—early popularist democrats who had failed in their efforts to wrest the franchise from Cromwell. The Levellers had argued that people were not bound to obey laws in whose making they had no voice. Locke resuscitated this argument and developed it into the powerful concept of the "consent of the governed," a bulwark of all subsequent demands for political liberty. To Locke, civil peace is not provided by a despotic Hobbesian sovereign but by laws freely agreed to by those laws' subjects. Hence, the law is seen as protecting liberty (after all, Locke argued, only a criminal feels coerced by a just law). Moreover (and here Locke earns his Libertarian spurs) "whenever law ends, tyranny begins." What follows from that assertion is crucial: if a king goes beyond the law, he goes beyond the authority vested in him by the consent of the governed. When that happens the people have a right to rebel, a point enthusiastically embraced by Jefferson and his fellow signers of the Declaration of Independence. (Jefferson's rejection of many other major concepts of Libertarianism, and the fact that Libertarians have been the most virulent critics of the Natural Rights orientation of the Declaration, are points to which we shall return.)

Still, Locke's definition of freedom, as "a liberty to follow my own will in all things where the [law] prescribes not," leaves unresolved the problem of obeying unjust laws. After all, the people might consent to a law that abridges the freedom of a minority, a problem Locke failed to anticipate. (Indeed, the problem of the tyranny of the majority would not be fully resolved for over a century, until James Madison showed in his "Federalist Paper Number 10" how pluralism protects the rights of minorities, as we see in Chapter 4.)

Locke also did not fully anticipate the anarchists' objection that all laws abridge freedom. Doesn't the very entering into the social contract cause us to abandon our natural liberty? Not in the least, according to Jean Jacques Rousseau, who addressed himself to this, the fundamental problem inherent in the notion of the social contract: "The problem is to find a form of association which will defend and protect [with] the whole common force the person and goods of each associate, and in which each, while uniting himself with all, may still obey himself alone, and remain as free as before." In other words, how can people retain their Natural Right to freedom if they have contracted to live under the laws of the state? Rousseau's solution to that puzzle was ingenious: he argued that no sane person would ever agree to live under civil law if that contract entailed turning over Natural Rights to the whims of some ham-fisted Leviathan. He asks, in effect, what kind of idiot would voluntarily agree to sell himself into slavery? In fact, Rousseau argued, answering his own question, all that is given up in joining civil society is the questionable right to self-preservation, and he assures us that the collective protection of the community is worth much more than the do-it-yourself variety. In sum, when one obeys a law that is in one's self-interest, one hasn't given up any freedom worth the name. The best part of the bargain is that everyone else has agreed to the same deal. "Finally, each man, in giving himself to all, gives himself to nobody; and as there is no associate over whom he does not acquire the same right as he yielded others over himself, he gains an equivalent for everything he loses, and an increase of force for the preservation of what he has."

To Rousseau, then, the issue is not freedom *from* government, but freedom *under* government. He directly contradicts himself elsewhere when he complains of the lack of true freedom in civil society; this contradiction aside, though, he affirms that under a legitimate government one is free even if the majority makes a law that is contrary to one's wishes. After all—and Locke concurred on this point—when one has given one's consent to majority rule, the law is thus "of one's own making" even if one disagrees with it!

J. S. Mill didn't buy it, or at least not all of it. While he approved of Locke's and Rousseau's efforts to ensure the liberty of the many from the despotism of kings and oligarchies, he found their ideas insufficient when it came to protecting the rights of minorities. During the height of Victorian social repression Mill called for the protection of individuality (paradoxically, this social repression occurred contemporaneously with the full flowering of economic laissez faire in England). In arguing the necessity to preserve freedom of thought, expression, conscience, tastes, pursuits, and association, Mill put the case in a timeless fashion. "The only freedom which deserves the name is that of pursuing our own good in our own way, so long as we do not attempt to deprive others of theirs, or impede their efforts to obtain it."

Mill's philosophy does not rest on a premise of selfishness. He took the high moral ground that what is good for society must be the foremost concern, and concluded optimistically that in most cases what is good for the individual is good for all of society in the long run, for "in proportion to the development of his individuality, each person becomes more valuable to himself, and therefore more valuable to others." (This concept has important parallels to the economic premises of Adam Smith, as we shall see.) Mill's famous dictum that the individual ought to be free to do whatever he or she wants as long as it doesn't hurt anyone else (or, in popular parlance, "your right to swing your fist stops at the point of my nose") constitutes a general principle that protects both the individual and society.

This principle operationalizes Kantian ethics. Kant had written, "Freedom is independence of the compulsory will of another; and in so far as it can co-exist with the freedom of all according to a universal law, it is the one sole, original inborn right belonging to every man in virtue of his humanity." (Kant's position differs from that of Locke and Rousseau, who had posited, in addition to the right to liberty, a limited Natural Right to property—a central concern to which we also shall return.) Modern Libertarianism finds its moral justification in Kant's humanistic belief that people are ends, not means. The consequences of this position are far-reaching, and form the underpinnings of such modern notions as "It degrades the dignity of the individual to make him or her subservient to the will of the state" and "The government that governs least governs best." Such modern writers as Ayn Rand also use the arguments of Kant (and Mill) as moral justification for radical individualism.

The Kantian belief that all people have an equal right to

freedom is also the entry point into another modern Libertarian principle: The equal right to freedom constitutes the full extent of human equality; all other equalities are unwarranted and unjust. To fully appreciate the import of that point, we now turn to the second domain of freedom.

Economic Liberty

The second, and more problematic, sphere of liberty was revealed to a ready world by the moral philosopher Adam Smith in 1776. Smith's intent was to discredit the prevailing economic system of mercantilism, which was based on the belief that, because wealth consists solely of gold and silver, it was incumbent on European nations to run a positive balance of trade with their colonies, the deficit to be made up in the transfer of those precious metals. Smith demolished this notion with a single, brilliant thunderbolt: in good Enlightenment fashion, he made the individual the center of his new system. "The consumer is king," he declared in *The Wealth of Nations*. He then called attention to the unfortunate fact that "the interest of the consumer is almost always sacrificed to that of the producer" and that government, interfering in the market by granting mercantilist monopolies, abetted this injustice. Smith then advanced the radical notion that it was free competition, among countries and among producers, that truly led to the increase of a nation's wealth. His greatest intellectual contribution was the concept of the market—the law of supply and demand—by which "the invisible hand" of competition would force greedy, self-interested, collusion-minded producers to work unwittingly to the maximum benefit of society.

Smith's notion of economic individualism aiding society so nicely dovetailed with Mill's similar notion about the collective benefits of social and political individualism that the two merged into a single theory of Libertarianism in the late nineteenth century. (Lost in that merger was the fact that the application of marketplace ethics to the social arena would have been reprehensible to the moralistic Smith, and that Mill had written specifically that "the principle of individual liberty is not included in the doctrine of Free Trade." Like Smith, Mill believed in economic laissez faire; he, too, argued that free markets were not only efficient but also curtailed the power of the state. But he added the proviso that the laws of economics have to do only with the *production* of goods and services. The other end of the process, *the distribution of wealth*, "depends on the laws and customs of society." For this socialistic heresy, the author of *On Liberty* is denied a place in the modern pantheon of Libertarian heroes!)

The two threads of Libertarianism, the political and the economic, were joined by Herbert Spencer in Britain and William Graham Sumner in America shortly before the end of the nineteenth century. Sumner advanced four propositions: Justice equals perfect liberty; perfect liberty equals economic liberty; economic liberty is founded on private property; and property accrues to the most deserving individuals.

> What we mean by liberty is civil liberty, or liberty under law; and this means the guarantee that a man shall not be interfered with while using his own powers for his own welfare. It is, therefore, a civil and political status; and that nation has the freest institutions in which the guarantee of peace for the laborer and security for the capitalist are the highest.

Sumner was a strong proponent of the U.S. Constitution, and in particular Madison's Bill of Rights, which he viewed as the greatest safeguard ever created by humankind for the protection of civil liberties and private property. At the same time, he bitterly denounced as "devoid of sense" the Jeffersonian principles of Natural Rights enunciated in the Declaration of Independence. We will return to this conflict; for now, we should note that Sumner's Libertarian philosophy was dominant in the United States for the first quarter of this century, went into partial eclipse for the next quarter, and has enjoyed a lengthy resurgence in the post-World War II era. (In Europe, particularly in Britain, Libertarianism held sway for much of the nineteenth century, and is just now enjoying renewed popular acceptance.)

The postwar resurgence of Libertarianism was due, in great part, to the influence of the Austrian-American economist, Friedrich von Hayek. A major theme in Hayek's writings is that the greatest accomplishments of civilization—economic, technological, and social—result not from design but from unplanned patterns of competition. No government can process all the information out of which the market creates "spontaneous order." Worse, when government attempts to do so, it amasses authority at the expense of individual freedom. Every governmental action designed to impose order, through planning, regulation, or redistribution of income, amounts to the laying of a brick on "the path to serfdom." Indirectly, Hayek's work provided the rationale for the policies of Margaret Thatcher and Ronald Reagan, through its influence on all aspects of contemporary Libertarian economics, from monetarism to development economics. For example, today Libertarian economists argue that successful development of Third World economies can only be accomplished by the free play of markets. They claim that attempts by governments to plan development will backfire (witness the relative failures of India and most of Africa), while laissez faire policies have led to the relative eradication of poverty in the Four Dragons of East Asia.

Finally, there is one additional form of economic freedom whose value is becoming universally recognized: the freedom of the entrepreneur to fail. Shortly after the conclusion of World War II, another Austrian-American economist, Joseph Schumpeter, called attention to the fact that the innovations of entrepreneurs were the true source of the dynamism of capitalism. He thus advocated free markets because the ongoing process of new business start-ups, and unsuccessful business failures, provides a "perennial gale of creative destruction" that benefits all society in the form of new products, services, and jobs.

By this point the reader may have perceived a Western bias to this outline. With regard to freedom, such cultural selectivity is unavoidable. As Japan's Doi Takeo explains, the Western concepts of freedom are unknown in traditional Japanese and Chinese thought. Takeo posits that a reaction to the slavery that underpinned the ancient Greek economy was what led to the West's understandable emphasis on individual freedom. Since slavery never existed in Asia, there was no such need "for asserting the superiority of the individual." There are increasing demands in Asia today, though, for Western-style liberties. As the world becomes homogenized, with the internationalization of markets and the use of mass telecommunications, Western values are spreading to those nations that are adopting Western-style democracies, economies, technologies, and especially popular culture. Asians are finding that they can't have Michael Jackson without John Stuart Mill.

Contemporary Libertarianism

In his 1962 book *Capitalism and Freedom*, Milton Friedman promoted "the role of competitive capitalism—the organization of the bulk of economic activity through private enterprise operating in a free market—as a system of economic freedom and a necessary condition for political freedom." Over the next three decades, Friedman and his University of Chicago colleagues (students and disciples of Hayek) developed a thoroughgoing critique of post–New Deal society based on principles derived from Locke, Smith, and Sumner that "emphasized freedom as the ultimate goal and the individual as the ultimate entity in society." In the tradition of Kant, these modern Libertarians acknowledge only one Natural Right, the right to liberty, to which all humans are equally entitled. (In all other matters justice requires *inequality*, because humans are born with different productive capacities.)

Libertarians, following Smith and Summer, believe that concentration of power in the hands of the state is the greatest threat to individual freedom. They believe private property and market mechanisms are essential for political liberty, since both limit the power of the state. In fact, following Smith, the market is doubly attractive to them: first, it is self-regulating, removing the need for government interference; second, it leads to the most efficient allocation of goods and services, offering incentives for productivity, innovation, and economic growth—thus providing the population with the highest possible standard of living.

Most important, the market pays obeisance to only one master: king consumer. This consumer is a rational actor, *homo economicus*, who relentlessly pursues his or her own self-interest. While the consumer may have her own ethical beliefs, they are her own business and her business alone: to Libertarians, morality is an individual matter and not a social or corporate concern. The proper role of government is simply to preserve law and order, provide for defence, and enforce contracts; the role of the corporation is limited to maximizing shareholder profits. The voluntary actions of free individuals will take care of the rest.

In this view, justice is achieved through the mechanism of competition. Again following the logic of Smith, each enterprise, by pursuing profit maximization, will provide the goods and services society needs at the price it is willing to pay. Those individuals who are the most talented, work hardest, or make the greatest contribution to society will be justly rewarded. The good society, defined by Libertarians as deriving from "the sum total of individual preferences," will be realized through the auspices of freedom.

Believing these things, Libertarians contend that government in modern America is too big. (It is responsible for some 37 percent of total spending in the economy, according to a 1990 OECD reckoning.) Actively engaged in regulation and planning, government not only stifles competition and discourages innovation, it compromises freedom. In particular, excessively high rates of taxation go to support activities the government should not be involved in: welfare state programs that are both unjust and inefficient because under them the bureaucrat, not the individual, is king. Consequently, Libertarians wish to secure the good society by means of deregulation, privatization of government agencies, decentralization of authority, putting tax money back in the hands of consumers, and encouraging competition—in short, by limiting the sphere of government to those few measures to secure personal and property rights that Locke claimed require collective as opposed to individual action.

In essence, the modern Libertarian, like her historical forerunners, believes that voluntary cooperation among self-interested individuals is the only alternative to tyrannical coercion by the state. In the words of Friedman, there is "no example in time or place of a society that has been marked by a large measure of political freedom . . . that has not also used something comparable to a free market to organize the bulk of economic activity." That point is the base line from which all contemporary debates about the good society begin.

≣ Equality

The idea of equality is of even more recent origin than the modern concept of liberty, although as we have seen, the idea of *inequality* is ancient. In the fourth century B.C., Aristotle posited a natural hierarchy of the human race, with men by nature superior to women, and freemen by nature superior to slaves. In other words, some were born to rule, others to be ruled. The proof of this natural inequality was there for all to

observe: Aristotle pointed to the obvious fact that women be-
haved in a womanly way, tending to the home and not participating in politics like men, and that slaves' behavior was slavish
in the extreme, not at all like the self-confidence of freemen.
Ipso facto, social inequality is natural.

For nearly two thousand years, Aristotle's view remained
uncontested. All forms of social inequality—of caste, class,
race and gender—were seen as given by nature, thus unques-
tioned and unquestionable. (Plato was one notable and ironic
exception; that most outspoken critic of social and political
equality asserted the equality of the sexes. In *The Republic*,
Socrates argues that if the difference between men and women
"consists only in women bearing and begetting children, this
does not amount to proof that a woman differs from a man in
respect to the sort of education she should receive." Furthermore, "the guardians and their wives ought to have the same
pursuits" since "the gifts of nature are alike diffused in both.")

Doubtless the impulse toward equality has roots that date
to the dawn of human history, but modern Egalitarianism had
to wait until 1762, when Rousseau refuted Aristotle's views of
slavery in *The Social Contract*. Rousseau argued that the ancient
"took the effect for the cause . . . if there be slaves by nature,
it is because there have been slaves against nature. Force made
the first slaves . . ." Rousseau thus introduced the concept of
"acquired differences." To him, the observed inequalities of
humankind were the result of *nurture*—that is, how people
were treated—as opposed to the Aristotelian view that the
cause was *nature*—what we would today call genetic factors.
Over time, Rousseau attracted a small number of adherents to
his position—most notably Marx, Robert Owen, and, to some
degree, Jefferson—but Aristotelians remained the vast majority.

Until the twentieth century, only J. S. Mill among major
political philosophers put forth a case for the equality of
women. Mill's wife, Harriet Taylor, advanced the argument in

Rousseauesque terms, declaring that women were inferior because that was the way men treated them. (She also, far ahead of her time, extended that argument to the arena of racial equality.) A half century later, Virginia Woolf advanced the Mills' argument inventing a fictional sister of Shakespeare. Woolf showed how the talents of this brilliant woman would have been lost to the world because she would have been assumed incapable of being a playwright, and denied the opportunity to prove she could be one. At about the same time, G. B. Shaw took up the feminist cause with a Platonic argument, advising the audiences of *St. Joan* to discard "sex partialities and their romance" and to see "woman as the female of the human species."

Shaw's argument for the unity of the species had almost been made in the seventeenth century by Hobbes, who, following in Aristotle's footsteps, had sought the way to distinguish humankind from the beasts. While arguing that the distinction is rooted in the human species' unique language and reasoning abilities, Hobbes failed to take the next step in the logic and to conclude that these similarities among all humans are far more important than the few observable gender or racial differences found between them. Of course, at the time Hobbes was writing, there was no question of the equality of the entire human race. The issue of that day (advanced by the Levellers in 1647) was whether all British men should be considered equal for the purposes of the franchise. Full political equality—universal suffrage—would take another three hundred years for realization in the English-speaking world.

The definition of who was a full and equal member of the human race, thus entitled to a say in government, expanded at a glacial pace in America and England: Complete male suffrage was granted in Britain in 1863; blacks were enfranchised in America in 1870; female suffrage occurred in Britain in 1914 (in the United States, six years later). The political equality of all Americans was not constitutionally guaranteed until the poll tax was outlawed by the Twenty-ninth Amendment in 1964.

Today, the suffrage issue is moot in the Western world. The sticking point that made the extension of the franchise so controversial for so many centuries is still alive, though, and remains at the core of the continuing Egalitarian cause: the struggle for greater economic equality. Without it, Egalitarians say, there can be no true political equality.

Property and Economic Inequality

Rousseau believed that the origin of inequality lay in the hallowed right to property. He believed this right "is the most sacred of all rights of citizenship," but complained that the great proprietors were deaf to an important question of social justice: "Do you not know that a number of your fellow-creatures are starving for want of what you have too much of?" Rousseau thus became the first to advance the case for economic equality. (Plato had called for a form of communism among the guardians in *The Republic*, not for social equality but to eliminate envy and ambition among the ruling class. Aristotle scored Plato on this, suggesting instead that the ideal was for all men to moderate voluntarily their thirst for wealth. As for Socrates' suggestion "that the wives of our guardians are to be common, and their children are to be common," Aristotle sensibly noted that "the scheme, taken literally, is impracticable.")

Rousseau seems to have believed that there once had been basic economic equality among primitive humankind. Indeed, Hobbes, Locke, Smith, and Marx all, like Rousseau, assumed that material things were held in common in the state of nature. They also believed that whatever property one of these primitives had removed from the state of nature was rightfully his. In Locke's famous words, "Whatsoever, then, he removes out of the state that Nature hath provided and left it in, he hath mixed his labor with it, and joined to it something that is his own, and thereby makes it his property."

In thus advancing the right of ownership, Locke's Labor Theory of Property laid the groundwork for the more controversial Labor Theory of Value, which, in the hands of Karl Marx, would prove to be a lethal intellectual weapon. (When Marx was young his father sat him on his knee and read to him from Locke.) Building on Locke's idea that by mingling one's labor with property one makes it one's own, Marx concluded that all property must be "congealed labor," hence the value of a product is equal to the labor time expended in its production. (To oversimplify: the value of the table a carpenter takes two days to make is twice that of the chair she makes in one day).

In and of itself, this theory did not become controversial until it was discredited by Alfred Marshall in 1890. In fact, every economist in the eighteenth and nineteenth centuries—including Smith, David Ricardo, and Mill—believed in the Labor Theory of Value. Where the theory became particularly problematic was in the application of the peculiarly Marxian notion of "surplus value." Marx argued that capitalists paid workers only a subsistence wage and not the true value of their labor, pocketing the difference as surplus value (what we call profit). This unjust act of expropriation, the alienation by the capitalist of what rightly belonged to workers by virtue of their labor, became the moral justification for the world's first full-blown demand for economic equality. On this point, Mortimer Adler notes that Marx's theory was, in fact, based on a misreading of Locke. Adler points to a passage in which Locke indicates that the profits fairly earned by a capitalist are as rightly his as are the returns to labor. (It is intriguing to picture little Karl nodding off just as his daddy got to this passage. One wonders if the world would have been spared a century of Marxist mischief had young Karl not had an exhausting day playing skittles with the other kids in the streets of Trier.)

Marx goes on to posit class warfare between the 10 percent who possess the means of production and the 90 percent from whom this property was wrongfully expropriated. He predicted that this struggle would end with the "expropriation of the expropriators." Then, in place of capitalism, a classless society would arise in which the collective ownership of all property would assure true equality, and the necessities of life would be distributed according to the Egalitarian principle, "From each according to his ability, to each according to his needs."

In expounding this theory, Marx found himself, for one brief moment, the guiding light of the entire Egalitarian movement. But no sooner had he laid down this law (and "law" it was, in a deterministic sense) than an irreconcilable split occurred in the movement. On one front Marx and Engels were at the vanguard of the communists seeking the violent destruction of capitalism; on the other, democratic socialists sought to use the newly won franchise as the means to reform that same system.

Democratic Egalitarianism

Rousseau's Egalitarian proclivities earned him a permanent niche in the Libertarian Hall of Shame. He was not quite a communist, though, as we see in his proposed solution to the problem of economic inequality.

> Since it is plainly contrary to the law of nature . . . that the privileged few should gorge themselves with superfluities while the starving multitude are in want of the bare necessities of life . . . one of the most important functions of government [is] to prevent extreme inequalities of fortunes; not by taking away wealth from its possessors, but by depriving all men of means to accumulate it; not by building asylums for the poor, but by securing the citizens from becoming poor.

In this call for what became known as the welfare state, Rousseau, not Marx, would have the last word. (Curiously the policy implications of Rousseau's welfare state were first spelled out by Thomas Paine, hero of the American Revolution and author of that famous plea for liberty, *Common Sense*. In the 1790s, Paine put forward proposals for a guaranteed annual income to be funded by an inheritance tax on large estates.) Democratic Egalitarianism became a movement that would run from the Enlightenment to this day. The intent of democratic socialists during this entire period has been Rousseau-esque: not to confiscate the property of the rich but to guarantee the necessities of life to the poor.

The question democratic Egalitarians have repeatedly put to society is this: Can one have political independence without economic independence? Even nonsocialists have worried about that question: Mill, Madison, Benjamin Franklin, and Alexis de Tocqueville all felt that vast wealth conferred undue political power. As Alexander Hamilton put it, "A power over a man's subsistence amounts to a power over his will." To address this issue, Horace Mann argued that political equality demands equality of educational opportunity. "If one class possesses all the wealth and the education, while the residue of society is ignorant and poor, it matters not by what name the relation between them may be called; the latter, in fact and in truth, will be the servile dependents and subjects of the former."

Henry George advanced Mann's argument one step further. In his view, extreme inequality would lead to economic disaster for all of society. George said there could be no material progress if social energies were continually wasted in class conflict. He concluded that the gap between the rich and the poor must be closed by income redistribution. While he felt that the Marxist solution of total equality was unjust and inefficient, George nonetheless concluded that progress required

"an association of equality." There is, of course, a major difference between Mann's call for "equality of educational opportunity" and George's for greater "equality of economic conditions." Both authors were committed to democratic means to
the ends they proposed; the former did not require individuals
in one class to sacrifice for those in the other, while the latter
required governmental action to that end—coercion, in fact, in
the form of nonvoluntary taxation.

By what right may society take the property of those who
have earned their wealth through honest means? The justification for society helping the have-nots turns on Jefferson's notion that every individual has an inalienable right to "life,
liberty and the pursuit of happiness." By the Natural Right to
pursue happiness Jefferson meant that every individual is entitled to make all she can of her life. By virtue of one's
humanity—if you will, by virtue of the Kantian principle that
every individual is "an end in himself"—*everyone* has a right to
pursue self-development. While equality of opportunity is thus
a necessary condition for the pursuit of happiness, for many
individuals it is insufficient. How can children who are un-
healthy, undernourished, ill-clothed, and poorly sheltered take
advantage of opportunities to learn and succeed?

Jeffersonians argue that they can't, and conclude that Natural Rights must extend beyond the right to liberty (as granted
by Libertarians) to include access to the minimal necessities of
livelihood that would permit everyone to take advantage of
equality of opportunity. In the eyes of Libertarians like Sumner, of course, "this concept lends itself to the most vicious
kind of social dogmatism, for if a man has natural rights, the
reasoning is clear up to the finished socialistic doctrine that a
man has a natural right to whatever he needs, and that measure
of his claims is the wishes he wants fulfilled." Not so, said the
Jeffersonian John A. Ryan in 1906: While everyone is entitled
to the basic *needs* to pursue happiness, no one has an unlimited
right to whatever he or she *wants*. As Ryan explained, "Again,

the right to liberty and property are not absolute in the sense that the individual may have as much of those goods as he pleases and do with them as he pleases, but inasmuch as within reasonable limits—which are always determined by the essential needs of personal development—these rights are sacred and inviolable."

A corollary to this proposition is that the state has a claim on the property of all citizens to insure the access of the poorest to the pursuit of happiness. Thus, the difficult practical questions facing democratic Egalitarians are these: "To how much is one entitled for self-development?" and "How much is the state entitled to claim from the haves in order to enable the have-nots to pursue their inalienable rights?"

Benjamin Franklin saw no limit to the state's claim. "Private property . . . is a creature of society and is subject to the calls of that society whenever its necessities shall require it, even to its last farthing." If Franklin's position sounds extreme—and no question it was, especially coming as it did from one who was a highly successful entrepreneur and land speculator!—some twentieth-century Egalitarians would agree with him. For example, in the 1970s, the Social Democratic government in Sweden placed a marginal tax of 101 percent on the highest incomes.

Most Egalitarians do not go nearly as far as Franklin and the Swedish Social Democrats in pursuing social equality. More typical is the position of the late British Labourite R. H. Tawney, who argued that differences in income are just in that they are necessary as motivation for effort. What is *unjust*, he wrote, is the coexistence within one society of two classes of people living at different levels of civilization; for example, the nonworking British aristocracy luxuriating in regal splendor cheek-by-jowl with an impoverished working class barely surviving in Dickensian squalor. To Tawney, then, the good society "invokes, in short, a large measure of economic equality— not necessarily in the sense of identical incomes, but of equality of environment, of access to education and the means of civilization, of security and independence, and of the social consideration which equality in these matters usually carries with it."

In the United States, Abraham Lincoln, Theodore and Franklin Roosevelt, and Martin Luther King, Jr. each argued, in turn, that the time had come to finally make good on the provision of the Natural Rights promised by Jefferson. In his 1944 State of the Union message, FDR declared the necessity for a second Bill of Rights, an economic guarantee to complement the existing political document, because "necessitous men are not free men. People who are hungry and out of a job are the stuff of which dictatorships are made." Roosevelt's proposal went nowhere, and nearly half a century later, Jefferson's promise is still just that. Libertarians, for their part, say that America's continuing rejection of the notion of economic rights is based on the soundest reason in the world: The extension of Natural Rights poses a threat to liberty.

The Painful Trade-Off

In 1835 Tocqueville wrote, "It is possible to imagine an extreme point at which freedom and equality would meet and blend." Indeed, even Libertarians concede that political equality and political liberty are perfectly compatible; moreover, political liberty and equality of opportunity are fraternal. As Tocqueville noted, though,

> Although men cannot be absolutely equal unless they are absolutely free; and consequently equality, pushed to its furthest extent may be confounded with freedom, yet there is good reason for distinguishing the one from the other. The taste which men have for liberty and that which they feel for equality are, in fact, two different things; and I am not afraid to add that, amongst democratic nations, they are two unequal things.

In fact, Tocqueville says, liberty and equality are antagonistic. He suggests that the "passion for equality penetrates on every side into men's hearts, expands there and fills them entirely." The potent mixture of equality and democracy worried him greatly. In a nation where the masses are enfranchised, he says they will pursue equality at the expense of liberty, and even if one demonstrates "freedom escaping their grasp" they will be "blind" to it, "or, rather, they can discern but one object to be desired in the universe." Tocqueville feared that this overriding passion for equality could lead to totalitarianism.

Tocqueville's reading of the incompatibility of liberty and equality had been anticipated by the formidable South Carolina Senator John C. Calhoun, who warned in 1831 that to "make equality of *condition* essential to liberty would be to destroy both liberty and progress." Seventy years later, Sumner asserted that equality of condition would lead to the death of individual freedom because such equality could not be achieved without a totalitarian socialist government. Sumner went so far as to identify the individual whose Egalitarian ideas most threatened the liberty of Americans: Thomas Jefferson. "The notion of natural rights is destitute of sense," he wrote, and fired off a warning to Americans that they must shake themselves free of their Jeffersonian sentimentalism—he called it "socialism"—and face up to the existence of a terrible trade-off: "Let it be understood that we cannot go outside of this alternative: liberty, inequality, survival of the fittest; not liberty, equality, survival of the unfittest. The former carries society forward and favors all its best members; the latter carries society downwards and favors its worst members."

Nearly every leading thinker in the last century believed that society faces an inescapable choice between liberty and equality. In certain circles today it is still the received wisdom that each increment of equality gained in a society will bring the loss of an increment of liberty, and vice versa. Two examples illustrate the trade-off. First, in the most relentlessly Egalitarian modern society, Maoist China, where the ratio of the incomes of the highest-paid to those of the lowest-paid was as low as four to one, this relative equality was achieved at the cost of a considerable loss of liberty—the confiscation of property, censorship, banishment, and even death to dissenters. Second, in the most Libertarian of modern societies, Victorian England, liberty was achieved at the cost of enormous economic inequalities; the ratio of richest to poorest incomes was as high as one hundred thousand to one. We can see why liberty versus equality has been called the most painful trade-off of modern society.

In light of the near consensus on the existence of this trade-off, the time has come to refer to our compass card. As expected, we find liberty and equality depicted as opposite values, implying that there is a trade-off to be made between these two values. Yet they are found on the same axis. Could it be that, in some way or ways, the two opposed values may be related (or fraternal, to use Tocqueville's word)? Since we could see the two values as running together in the middle of the compass, is it possible, as Tocqueville (perhaps inconsistently) claims, that "equality pushed to its furthest extent may be confounded with freedom"?

This idea makes sense only if freedom and equality are viewed as values with varying degrees of intensity rather than as absolute values found only at the extreme poles. We have noted at least two instances that seem to support the former interpretation: neither equality of *opportunity* nor equal rights to liberty entail trade-offs between liberty and equality. The same might be said for the civil rights outlined in the U.S. Bill of Rights; for instance, equality *before the law* poses no threat to liberty. Admittedly, other possibilities for reconciling liberty and equality are not as easy to construct, as we find with the threats to liberty that are posed by taxation to provide the economic wherewithal for the *exercise* of equality of opportunity, and for the *exercise* of equality before the law. Nonetheless, we also should admit into evidence the following: the author of the most influential contemporary proposal for a negative income tax—in effect, for a guaranteed annual income—is not an Egalitarian but that quintessential Libertarian, Milton Friedman!

Friedman's inconsistency on this score would have appeared perfectly logical to J. S. Mill, who wrote, "The social problem of the future [is] how to unite the greatest liberty of action, with a common ownership in the raw materials of the globe, and an equal participation of all in the benefits of combined labor." By "combined labor" he meant the combination of labor and capital, both of which, in proper Lockean fashion, are entitled to a share in the fruits of production. In advocating what might on first glance appear to be Marxist redistribution, Mill insisted that he "repudiated with the greatest energy that tyranny over the individual which most Socialistic systems are supposed to involve." But he felt that the threat of collectivist authoritarianism was a red herring in such overwhelmingly Libertarian societies as Britain and the United States. In such nations, the real threat to liberty comes from the presence of idle, impoverished masses—and from a class of idle rich. Mill looked forward to a time when "the rule that they who do not work shall not eat will be applied not to paupers only, but impartially to all; when the division of the produce of labor, instead of depending, as in so great a degree it does now, on the accident of birth, will be made by concert on an acknowledged principle of justice." Mill concluded that the existence of a large class of poor people was not natural but, in fact, the product of social institutions: changing the distribution of income would do no violence to the laws of economics. While "the Production of Wealth" depends on the "real laws of nature"—that is, the efficient production of wealth is governed by Smith's invisible hand—in contrast, "the modes of its Distribution depend on human will." In sum, to Mill the democratic redistribution of wealth entailed no real trade-offs with either liberty or economic efficiency.

Contemporary Egalitarianism

Along with the recent discrediting of communism, there has been a parallel eclipse of democratic Egalitarianism in most Western nations. The non-Marxist John Rawls still propounds his Egalitarian "difference principle" that "All social values are to be distributed equally unless an unequal distribution" is to the advantage of the least-advantaged group; but the reputation of democratic socialism has been tarnished by the manifest collapse of "the other" socialism. In fact, the last American president with true Egalitarian convictions was Lyndon Johnson, whose Great Society was, in part, the brainchild of his chairman of economic advisors, Arthur Okun, the last prominent American economist to advance a program based on Natural Rights. For the United States finally to make good on the Jeffersonian promise, Okun proposed a guaranteed income to the poorest families amounting to "one half the average income of American families."

Modern Egalitarians in the Okun mold believe that all citizens have inalienable rights, both political and economic. While they favor the market mechanism on the production side, like Mill they see the market as an imperfect means for the distribution of income. In particular, they see unjust disparities in what Tawney called "levels of civilization" within the same nation (for example, the shocking juxtaposition of Manhattan's Upper East Side with impoverished adjoining Harlem). American Egalitarians in the 1990s hold that such disparities are, if anything, growing worse instead of being reduced. As the result of the Libertarian policies of the 1980s, between 1973 and 1991 median household income in the United States remained flat, while the percentage of families living in poverty rose from 11.1 percent to 14.7 percent. In the 1980s alone, the share of the nation's total household income held by the top half of 1 percent rose from 24.1 percent to 29.1 percent.

Egalitarians argue that these disparities do not reflect legitimate differences in ability or willingness to work but are more like the random rewards of a slot machine. At best, one can say that the rewards in the market are too great for the winners and too small for the losers. Hence, Okun called for the creation of a true meritocracy in America; to achieve it he proposed that the government should remove all barriers to social mobility (in particular, racial and sex discrimination) and create a "level playing field" so that all citizens could truly partake of equality of opportunity.

Okun suggested that such opportunity does not exist in America. Since the rich can buy outstandingly better health care, legal protection and education, the unfettered market transgresses on basic human rights. Egalitarians also score the market for failing to provide enough public goods (schools, hospitals, shelter), for creating regional imbalances (Appalachian poverty versus Aspen affluence), and for putting too much power into the hands of corporate executives and other wealthy people who can buy political influence. The market is also said to encourage short-term thinking, which has led to the failure of corporations to reinvest, thus causing a loss of American jobs to foreign competition.

The agenda of American democratic Egalitarians includes a redistribution of wealth through progressive taxation (the introduction of a negative income tax, and reform of the social security and inheritance tax systems), and an increase in the domain of Natural Rights (through such means as national health insurance and a national education tuition fund, and extending the social safety net to include child care and parental leave). Their stated goal is to help the poor to escape dependency on welfare by giving them incentives to work.

Egalitarians stand for full and equal rights for women. After the right to vote was secured in 1920, women's rights were put on the back burner in America until Betty Friedan's consciousness-raising book *The Feminine Mystique* was published in 1963. The book launched the contemporary American women's movement, which to this day has not achieved its objective of full equality. Most controversially, Egalitarians favor strengthening affirmative action to guarantee equality of opportunity, not just for women but for minorities as well.

Many Egalitarians argue for the creation of national policies aimed at full employment. These would include the stimulation of job-creating investment by public sector spending on roads, bridges, transportation, and such high-technology projects as pollution treatment and optical fibre networks. Egalitarians favor trade policies that protect domestic workers from the vagaries of foreign governments' protectionist policies, and they would restore the bargaining power of unions as a further means of providing security to the working class. To prevent the disasters that threaten the security of the most vulnerable members of society, they would reregulate banks and savings and loans, and increase the regulation of foods, drugs and working conditions. This agenda is consistent with traditional Egalitarian desires to remove the economic injustices rooted in social class stratification. In recent years, however, so-called politically correct American Egalitarians have emphasized removing discrimination against people who share such nonclass characteristics as gender, age, race, ethnicity, sexual preference and physical disability. Because our focus is on the historical roots of America's philosophical differences, I have not attempted to bring this chapter up to date with an account of these latest unfoldings of Egalitarian thought. Daniel Bell has undertaken admirably the task of describing the numerous factions into which contemporary Egalitarians, Libertarians, Corporatists, and Communitarians have split in the last quarter century (see bibliography). Suffice it to say that an accurate description of the subdivisions found today among just politically correct Egalitarians would require a mind-boggling quantity of detail, little of which is directly useful to our enquiry.

Yet, these ideological evolutions call attention to the fact that American attitudes about equality continue to change over time as, indeed, do the attitudes we hold concerning all values. Moreover, such attitudes vary greatly among cultures and nations. A 1987–1988 Gallup poll revealed sharp variances in the relative importance that citizens of seven industrialized countries assigned to the values of equality and freedom (earlier research in less-developed countries found even greater differences among cultures). When asked the following question, "Which is more important, equality or freedom?", the percentage of Americans choosing freedom was highest among those polled, and the percentage of Americans choosing equality was lowest:

	Percent choosing	
	Equality	*Freedom*
United States	20	72
Britain	23	69
France	32	54
Italy	45	43
West Germany	39	37
Japan	32	37
Spain	39	36

The fact that Americans in general became decreasingly enthusiastic about the value of equality in the 1980s informs the agendas of the nation's two political parties and explains why neither party today advocates the brand of income redistribution found in most other industrialized nations. When the Gallup pollsters asked, "Is it government's responsibility to reduce economic differences?" the percentage of Americans responding Yes was lowest among the nations sampled:

Percent saying yes	
Italy	81
Hungary	77
Holland	64
Britain	63
West Germany	56
Australia	42
United States	28

Arthur Okun's original contribution to Egalitarianism was his practical recognition that the American public would never support FDR's Economic Bill of Rights as long as they believed that doing so would entail a loss of liberty. Tocqueville was wrong, according to Okun; liberty, not equality, is the "one object to be desired in the universe." Hence, Okun shifted the nature of the century-old debate, suggesting—in the tradition of Mill—that policies that provide true equality of opportunity pose no threat to liberty. Unlike Mill, however, he wrote that "The Big Trade-Off" in modern times is between "equality and efficiency." Okun's perspective continues to be shared by European social democrats. In 1991 Jacques Delors, the head of the European Economic Community, wrote, "Our union must be as efficient as the United States, but without falling into its errors. It must be deeply rooted in social justice and the welfare state . . ."

≡ Efficiency

There is a widespread desire for economic efficiency among citizens of modern nations. While that desire is not as self-evident as, say, the yearning for freedom or equality, there is nonetheless powerful evidence that the good society is often equated with efficiency. Reports emanating from the former U.S.S.R. and its former East European satellites indicate that low incomes, empty stores, and long queues for necessities were what led to the fatal erosion of confidence in the communist system. If these reports are true, then the dramatic abandonment of Marxist Egalitarianism has been due more to a desire for a higher standard of living than a love of liberty.

Economic efficiency—increasing the wealth of a nation through the most productive application of labor and capital—is a modern notion derived from Adam Smith's pathbreaking insights into the true sources of economic growth. Aristotle, however, and, more directly, Plato had laid the philosophical groundwork for Smith two millennia earlier. Aristotle advanced a pair of proto-Smithian concepts—the division of labor, and the notion that economic progress requires growth in the size of production units (that is, economies-of-scale); Plato anticipated the modern corporate state and even the modern business corporation. As we shall soon see, not only is the famous pin factory described in the opening pages of Smith's *Wealth of Nations* a Platonic organization, so is General Motors!

Plato was no friend of liberty or equality—at least, not as a modern democrat would use those terms. In *The Republic*, Plato's dramatic voice, Socrates, says that democracy creates a city "full of freedom and frankness, in which man may do and say what he likes. . . . Where such freedom exists, the individual is clearly able to order for himself his own life as he pleases." Such a state sounds agreeable to the modern Libertarian; to Socrates it was tantamount to anarchy. Worse, he thought, political liberty leads to political equality, a situation that is unjust because people are not, by nature, equal. "Liberty," Socrates says, "is full of variety and disorder, and dispenses a sort of equality to equals and unequals like." That might sound desirable to modern Egalitarians, but Socrates found democracy the second worst form of government, only one rung above tyranny.

The Platonic ideal was the "well-ordered state," a government characterized by "the rule of the few." Importantly, this ruling elite, or oligarchy, is not composed of hereditary aristocrats who owe their positions to birth, wealth, force, or the inclination to power. That is the stuff of tyranny, and Plato would have none of it. Instead, the guardians of his ideal Republic rule by force of their manifest "virtue." The characteristics of this leadership elite are their knowledge, wisdom, competence, talent, and ability. In short, Plato proposes a nondemocratic state that is nonetheless just and legitimate because it is a meritocracy in which the leaders practice "the science of government"—"among the greatest of all sciences," he tells us, "and most difficult to acquire." Because the mastery of this science is so rarely achieved, "any true form of government can only be supposed to be the government of one, two, or, at any rate, of a few . . . really found to possess the science."

Plato's elite rule not for themselves, but for the good of society as a whole (in this he anticipates the nineteenth-century utilitarianism we discuss later). Plato has Socrates say that the purpose of the Republic "is not the disproportionate happiness of any one class, but the greatest happiness of the whole." Socrates even states that many people will not like living in his Republic, but nonetheless they should appreciate that it provides what is best for the greatest number of the citizenry.

To what specific end, though, do the guardians rule the Republic? Plato talks about "virtue," "truth," and "order," but what these words might mean, other than the definitions the guardians themselves will apply in their selfless quest for the good society, he does not say. In the realm of economy, the rulers seem to be charged with providing a high standard of living, not for themselves, but for the ruled. When Socrates posits a mere subsistence economy for the Republic, another character in the dialogue, Glaucon, counters that this would only be "providing a city of pigs." Glaucon argues that people need much more than bare necessities for "the ordinary conveniences of life. People who are to be comfortable are accustomed to lie on sofas, and dine off tables, and they should have sauces and sweets in the modern style." Taking his clue from Glaucon, Socrates gets into the luxury provision business himself, describing a "state at fever heat" economically, one that doesn't stop with necessities "such as houses and clothes and shoes. The acts of the painter and embroiderer will have to be set in motion, and gold and ivory and all sorts of metal procured." While it seems clear that Socrates (and Plato) are personally averse to such conspicuous consumption, other characters in the dialogues wish to make the Republic "as great and as rich as possible." Plato's system of guardianship is nothing if not consistent with that end.

The guardians of the Republic might be seen as analogous to the managers of modern, publicly held corporations. These men and women hold their positions not by dint of ownership, heredity, force, or election. Instead, in theory at least, they are a meritocratic elite who sit atop their hierarchies thanks to their manifest virtue: their skill, talent, intelligence, experience and wisdom (as warranted by the possession of the MBA degree!). Corporate managers should be those found to be the most qualified to guide the organization in pursuit of the common good of its constituencies. Moreover, like Plato's guardians, they must sacrifice their personal self-interest in order to maximize the wealth of those they serve: the shareholders. (J. K. Galbraith calls this paradoxical self-sacrifice by professional profit maximizers "the approved contradiction.")

Inherent in Plato's scheme is the notion of hierarchy: Efficiency requires a division of labor; an orderly division requires a hierarchy based on ability; and people in a hierarchical system will be, by definition, stratified in classes. Plato was unapologetic about the anti-egalitarian, antidemocratic nature of his Republic. He agreed with Aristotle that inequality based on merit was how things should be run, and that, further, the state takes precedence over the individual. In Aristotle's view, "the state is by nature clearly prior to [superior to] the family and the individual." From classical Athens to the present day, all subsequent hierarchies have been justified in terms of their efficiency and the necessity of putting the organization ahead of the individual in order to achieve collective progress.

Hence, where the individual is the measure of liberty and equality, the focus of efficiency is the state or organization. The most extreme expression of this Corporatist view was advanced by Hobbes, who argued that humankind is willing to abandon its natural liberty and equality for the security of the state. He believed that individuals form a combination—literally, a corporation—in the guise of the Leviathan, which is superior to the individual and, in effect, "an artificial man, though of greater stature and strength than the natural, for whose protection and defense it was intended." (We recognize this idea today in the legal notion that a corporation is an "artificial person.")

The function of the Leviathan is to foster the safety necessary for economic progress. Despotic rule is preferable to natural freedom on the grounds of efficiency. In the state of nature

> there is no place for industry, because the fruit thereof is uncertain: and consequently no culture of the earth; no navigation; nor use of the commodities that may be imposted by the sea; no commodious buildings; no instruments of moving and removing such as require more force; no knowledge of the face of the earth; no account of time; no arts; no letters; no society.

While many modern Corporatists would part company with Hobbes on the granting of total power to a Leviathan for the collective good, they all accept his view that a well-ordered organization is the fount of progress, a necessity for the advance of civilization. Such organizations are, by definition, oligarchic. After demolishing the Leviathan (in the person of Charles I), Cromwell and his supporters did not turn to democracy. Instead, they argued that there is a natural aristocracy of rulers based on their ownership of land. A century later,

Edmund Burke, no lover of tyranny, advanced the principle of "virtual representation," in which the best interests of the disfranchised working class would be represented in Parliament by their economic betters, who were, by definition, also their superiors in talent and education. One of the greatest of all liberals, J. S. Mill, so believed in the value of an intellectual aristocracy that he advocated proportional voting weighted by the amount of schooling each individual had received. At about the same time, Tocqueville, too, wrote in a Platonic mode, "An aristocracy is infinitely more skillful in the science of legislation than democracy can ever be." Even the American founders feared "mobocracy." They sought to moderate the effects of democracy by empowering a leavening class of elected leaders who they hoped would be more reasonable and deliberative than the impassioned masses. According to Madison, the U.S. Constitution aims "to obtain for rulers men who possess most wisdom to discern, and most virtue to pursue, the common good of society." Although the basis of American representative rule—an elite elected by the people—is far different from the Cromwellian elite of landed aristocrats, to critics of Corporatism it amounts to the same thing: inequality. Corporatist society, whatever its form, is oligarchic. Said Marx: "The state is the executive committee of the ruling class."

Writing in China roughly at the same time as Plato and Aristotle, Confucius drew many of the same conclusions as the ancient Greeks, including the superiority of meritocratic oligarchy. Like Hobbes, Confucius was led to advocate such a form of government by his fear of disorder. Indeed, throughout history and across cultures, the dominant view has been that the only realistic alternative to anarchy on the one hand, and tyranny on the other, is benevolent despotism. Relatively few philosophers at any time or in any culture have placed much faith in the efficacy of another possibility: democracy.

The Science of Economic Efficiency

While hierarchy seems an essential feature of Corporatism, what truly distinguishes its ideology from both Libertarianism and Egalitarianism is its largely economic focus. As we shall see later, Smith was of two minds about his pin factory, finding it both useful for its efficiency and immoral for its social costs. The true Corporatist is concerned only with the efficiency side of the equation. The Corporatist agrees with Smith-the-economist when he writes that the goals of economic policy are, "first, to provide a plentiful subsistence for the people, or more properly to enable them to provide such a revenue or subsistence for themselves; and secondly, to supply the state or commonwealth with a revenue for public services." Like Plato, there is a hint here of a higher good: efficiency may be the means to some greater end. But that end is not made explicit, and the accent is heavy on the economic means. The aim, says Smith in the next breath, is "to enrich both the people and the sovereign." Perhaps in church we may think about the higher implications of what we do, but in the real world of affairs, it all comes down to "cheapness and plenty," Smith's concise statement of the intended results of efficiency.

The irony, of course, is that Smith was not a Corporatist. Not only was the prime concern of Smith-the-moralist the welfare of the individual, his analytical point of departure was the entrepreneur/owner, whom he saw as the basic productive unit in an economy. In sharp contrast, Corporatists not only focus on groups (as opposed to individuals), they see the motivation inherent in direct ownership as irrelevant to the question of efficiency. Publicly held corporations, state-private partnerships—even state ownership under certain circumstances—any of these can be made proper vehicles for the maximization of the nation's wealth. While Libertarians and Egalitarians may argue that wealth creation is a positive value in that a high standard of living is a *means* to greater liberty or equality, the true Corporatist is incorrigibly pragmatic. Men and women of practical mind have always been drawn to the position that economic efficiency (wealth creation) is a worthy *end* in itself. That quintessential realist, Samuel Johnson, said to Boswell upon reading Rousseau's call for equality, "Sir, you may make the experiment. Go into the street, and give one man a lecture on morality, and the other a shilling, and see which will respect you the most." Such cynicism aside, it seems wrong to dismiss the pursuit of efficiency as totally lacking in moral justification. As the former leaders of communist states have just learned, and as the current leaders of impoverished Third World nations must be aware, the efficient production and distribution of goods is not an insignificant moral value: it leads to employment, thus to the overall well-being of a nation. (If Dr. Johnson were alive today, he would ask Boswell if he would earn more respect in Ethiopia if he brought that country a General Motors plant or a democratic parliament.) Consequently, economic growth—the annual increase in GNP—has become the major measure of success in almost all modern nations, and the primary end of many governments.

In America, Alexander Hamilton successfully put economic efficiency on the national agenda. He believed the threat of war "will compel nations the most attached to liberty to resort for repose and security to institutions which have a tendency to destroy their civil and political rights. To be more safe, they at length become willing to run the risk of being less free." As Secretary of the Treasury during Washington's first administration, Hamilton sent Congress a "Report on Manufactures" in December 1791 that called upon the United States to abandon its agrarian bias and embrace industrialism. In order to increase national wealth, Hamilton advocated using the power of government to provide the infrastructure and other incentives needed for the establishment of modern textile factories in the United States. In putting forth this "national industrial policy," Hamilton argued that America would by means of a public-private partnership free itself of economic dependence on Europe. He attacked Adam Smith with his right hand, calling his laissez-faire approach to business hopelessly naive in a complex world of international cartels and government-supported industries, and Jefferson with his left, arguing that the Sage of Monticello was living in the past if he thought that agriculture could ever be as productive or profitable as manufacturing. Hamilton urged America to join the industrial revolution and follow Britain in the introduction of the cotton mill.

> In consequence of it, all the different processes for spinning cotton are performed by means of machines which are put in motion by water, and attended chiefly by women and children; and by a smaller number of persons, in the whole, than are requisite in the ordinary mode of spinning. And it is an advantage of great moment that the operations of this machine will continue, with convenience, during the night as well as through the day. The prodigious effect of such a machine is easily conceived.

Contrasting the productive, urban-based textile factory with the less-efficient, rural-based agricultural system favored by Jefferson, Hamilton concluded that the former offered numerous unique benefits:

> It is worthy of particular remark that, in general, women and children are rendered more useful, and the latter more early useful, by manufacturing establishments than they would otherwise be. Of the number of persons employed in the cotton manufactories of Great Britain, it is computed that four-sevenths, nearly, are women and children; of whom the greatest proportion are children, and many of them of a tender age.

In effect, Hamilton successfully advocated the importation of "dark, satanic mills" into the United States. A Faustian bargain was struck. The industrial revolution entailed an exchange of Jefferson's world of "virtuous, self-sufficient" farmers for the Dickensian world of grinding poverty in industrial cities—or, put positively, an exchange of what Marx had called "the idiocy of rural life" for a world of material progress. No one—not Marx, or Dickens—argued in the final analysis that the bargain was a bad one. It is difficult to find a serious author who does not admit that industrialism was a necessary stage in human progress. Even Jefferson ultimatley came around to a begrudging acceptance of manufacturing.

When Hamilton spoke in 1791 of making young children "more early useful," he was using the language of utilitarianism, which had been introduced two years earlier by the influential British philosopher and economist Jeremy Bentham. In fine Platonic fashion, utilitarians defined the good society as "the greatest good for the greatest number." J. S. Mill, who early in his career had been Bentham's prime disciple, came to question the justice of a system so bent on the scientific calculation of "the greatest good" (measured, quantitatively, in "utiles") that it ignored "the feelings" of the members of society, particularly those who were not part of "the greatest number." Mill came to conclude that a philosophy that could be used as justification for the employment of children could not be considered moral, no matter how scientific that justification was made to appear.

While Marx found modern industrial practices inherently evil because they were based on the exploitation of labor, he did extol industrial efficiency, devoting pages of the *Communist Manifesto* to praise of the capitalists who created the world of mass manufacturing and to the great increases in wealth that resulted. Lenin went much further in his enthusiasm. The Soviet leader was a great admirer of two exemplary American Corporatists of his era, Henry Ford and Frederick Winslow Taylor. So taken was Lenin with the efficiency of the assembly line that he sought a Ford truck plant for the U.S.S.R.; so struck was he with the possibilities of "scientific management" that he urged all Soviet factories to adopt Taylor's time-and-motion methods.

> The Soviet Republic must at all costs adopt all that is valuable in the achievements of science and technology. The possibility of building socialism will be determined precisely by our success in combining the Soviet government and the Soviet organization of administration with the up-to-date achievements of capitalism. We must organize in Russia the study and teaching of the Taylor system and systematically try it out and adapt it to our purposes.

Writing in an era when almost all businesses were small, local operations, Marx had predicted the development of giant, multinational corporations; Lenin outdid his master in the application of his ideas, surpassing even Western Corporatists in seeking economies-of-scale through the creation of the largest factories in the world in the Soviet Union.

By the early twentieth century, the value of efficiency had become dominant in the Western world, in communist and capitalist countries alike. Sociologists like Max Weber were even advocating the introduction of bureaucracy—formal, scientific hierarchy—in public and private institutions in the name of efficiency and the good society (the two concepts having become synonymous). By then, almost all economists had rejected as simplistic the Smithian philosophical approach to political economy in favor of Alfred Marshall's new scientific demonstration that efficiency could be defined as the point where the market "clears"—the point on a graph where supply and demand curves intersect. Perhaps even more influential from a Corporatist point of view was the work of the Italian Vilfredo Pareto, who early in this century introduced the concept of mathematical optimality. Pareto's mathematical formulae for determining the optimal allocation of resources in society, coupled with his Platonic belief in the superiority of elites, laid the basis for a modern school of Corporatist economics.

Credit Marshall or Pareto, the task for economists in the first seventy years of this century became removing the "imperfections" that blocked the achievement of market clearing. Paradoxically, where Smith and the Libertarians had posited that such imperfections were the result of government interference in the economy, Corporatists were not reluctant to use government as a tool to correct market outcomes. For example, J. M. Keynes worried that untoward savings could lead to a shortfall in demand—to market sub-optimization, as it were. His revolutionary idea was to have government shore up demand (through borrowing and spending) during severe recessions in order to make up the shortfall. In effect, through correcting market inefficiencies, he sought to achieve the ideal state of "full employment." Hamiltonian to his core, Keynes gave Libertarians fits.

Most singularly, the managers of *Fortune* 500 companies became Corporatists in the post–World War II era. They took their lead from the philosophy of engineering and managerial efficiency outlined by Alfred Sloan in his influential book *My Years with General Motors*. In its pages, Sloan uses the word efficiency (or its engineering and economic synonyms) as many as half a dozen times on a given page. Nowhere in the book, not even when describing GM's pivotal role in the U.S. war effort, does he make passing reference to liberty, equality, democracy, or any other social value.

The book describes what became the curriculum of American business schools in the decades that followed. Perhaps more important, as Asian nations adopted Western technology and Western-style economies during the same period, they gravitated toward the Corporatist pole, perhaps finding it compatible with Confucianism. Not until 1992 did a leading Japanese question that country's all-out embrace of Corporatism.

The chairman of the Sony corporation, Akio Morita, now argues that "Japanese companies should realize that they will no longer be allowed to continue their single-minded pursuit of economic efficiency and market success."

Corporatism has always attracted those, like Sloan, who have a scientific bent. One of its chief appeals is the absence of sentimentality, ideology, or superstition in its core beliefs. From the beginning, Corporatists have spoken the language of *Realpolitik*. During the Peloponnesian Wars, when the Athenians offered the Melians the choice between subjugation or total annihilation, they tried to persuade the hopelessly outmanned Melians to be "realists"—to accept the fact of life that might makes right and it was better to be Athenian than dead. The Athenians reasoned that the Melians should "aim at what is feasible" as opposed to what is idealistic. Machiavelli offered similar practical advice two thousand years later in *The Prince*, the first treatise to warrant the description "political science."

Like Machiavelli, Corporatists have little patience with the unscientific notion of Natural Rights in either its strong Egalitarian or weak Libertarian sense. Hardheaded Corporatists agree with Justice Bork (a Libertarian on most matters) that "no system of moral or ethical values has any objective or intrinsic validity of its own." They thus share today's dominant "positive law" position, which has been advanced over the years by such influential jurists as Holmes, Frankfurter, and Hand. What the belief comes down to is that there is no such thing as universal moral or philosophical truth; only what can be scientifically demonstrated can be called true. In the law of the marketplace, justice is represented by the given statutes at any time or place. When Corporatist executives disagree with a proposed government regulation, they do so not on the grounds of ethical justice or ideology, but on the pragmatic premise that what the law should be doesn't matter as much as that it should be the same for all their competitors, domestic and foreign.

On this and many other points, Corporatism and Libertarianism sound enough alike to cause many people to confuse them. For assistance in clarifying the differences between the two, we refer to our values quadrant. Efficiency is on a different axis on the compass from liberty and equality. Therefore, while efficiency differs from liberty, it cannot logically do so in the same way that equality does. Efficiency and liberty are not in direct opposition but are adjoining, and we find that the two values overlap in certain respects. For instance, both Libertarians and Corporatists celebrate the value of economic markets.

While the two positions thus overlap they are quite distinct. Libertarians value the economic effects of a free market but reserve their highest praise for systems that promote individualism, be it social, political, or economic. While Corporatists, too, value market mechanisms, they reserve their greatest praise for systems that promote the order and efficiency of the whole. Where Libertarians talk about entrepreneurship and individual preferences, the language of Corporatism is that of planning, technology, optimization, power, and organization. Thus Libertarians would favor the social, political, and economic system found in the American West during the Gold Rush, while Corporatists would prefer the system found in Lee Kuan Yew's post–World War II Singapore. Similarly, the behavior, attitudes and political preferences of American entrepreneurs tend to be Libertarian, while the comparable characteristics of professional managers of *Fortune* 500 firms tend to be Corporatist.

Similarly, while there is some blurring between values of efficiency and equality, Corporatists and Egalitarians' respective definitions of the good society are clearly distinct. Both groups favor planning and coordination between productive firms, unions, and government, and both are willing, on occasion, to sacrifice civil liberties in order to achieve what they consider higher ends. Nonetheless, their goals are dissimilar.

To the Corporatist, the good society is a well-ordered, efficient state with a high overall standard of living, whose benefits are distributed unequally on a meritocratic basis. In contrast, the Egalitarian defines the good society as a state in which all individuals have inalienable political and economic rights, and inequalities in the enjoyment of those rights are minimized as far as reasonably possible. No one should confuse the divergent goals of a Corporatist Singapore with those of an Egalitarian Denmark. (The distinctions between a state dedicated to efficiency and one dedicated to community are more difficult to draw, as we shall soon see in our discussion of Communitarianism, when we shall find that Plato was not simply a Corporatist!)

Contemporary Corporatism

The leading proponents of Corporatism today are probably Japanese and European business executives. While the leaders of large, publicly held American corporations also may be Corporatist in their thinking, their public pronouncements of that belief have been muted since the early 1980s, when they came under attack from Libertarians for a supposed lack of concern for shareholder rights; consequently, the clearest expressions of contemporary Corporatism come from the academic community. In the writings of Peter Drucker, Michael Porter, Herbert Simon, Lester Thurow, Robert Reich, and most notably J. K. Galbraith, we find descriptions of Corporatist behaviors and assumptions. Frequently, these descriptions are controversial, since the personal values of many of those authors are not Corporatist.

There is little controversy, however, over the fact that the highest Corporatist values are efficiency, productivity, international competitiveness, a high standard of living, and economic growth. In order to enhance the process of wealth creation, Corporatists believe in the necessity of economies-of-scale, particularly in industries competing in international markets. They argue that the world has become a single market financially and economically, and that competition in some industries is as much country versus country as company versus company. For this reason, Corporatists believe that governments must be advocates of corporations, not their adversaries, and should do all they can to advance the cause of domestic businesses in world markets. In particular, they ask government to secure a level playing field for global competition.

Corporatists are alarmed by what they see as the de-industrialization of America. They point to the loss of export markets for manufactured goods, the decline in productivity growth, and insufficient investment in new plants and technology. Since they believe that savings equal investment, they are particularly concerned by the fact that America's net savings rate is 4.7 percent (as opposed to 14.3 percent in Japan). They say this fact goes far to explain why U.S. investment as a share of GNP is lowest in the industrial world, why nondefense R & D expenditures are low and declining, and why net U.S. government investment in infrastructure is only 0.3 percent (compared to 5.7 percent in Japan).

Corporatists share the Libertarian belief that the market should be left to work wherever it works well, but they argue that Hamiltonian intervention is necessary in certain circumstances—for example, to give emerging high-tech companies an initial boost in competition with foreign government-sponsored companies. Corporatists do not reject outright such governmental interference in the economy as protection from "unfair" foreign competition, loans, bailouts, subsidies and R & D support.

Further, unlike Libertarians (who believe corporate executives' actions must be limited to maximizing profits for shareholders), Corporatists argue that, pragmatically, executives cannot ignore their responsibilities to other constituencies such as customers and employees, and that their broader social role is to serve society by providing goods, services, and technology. They dismiss the Libertarian economic model of self-regulating competition between numerous small producers as a naive "lemonade stand" view of the world. In today's highly concentrated and interdependent world markets, not all competitors are profit maximizers, thus Smith's invisible hand doesn't function. (For example, many competitors engage in dumping to build market share, and many executives engage not in profit maximizing but, instead, in "satisficing" in order to meet other, long-term goals.) Consequently, Corporatists argue that national antitrust laws are irrelevant and anachronistic, and should be relaxed to encourage the concentration and coordination needed to meet foreign competition. To put more long-term thinking into the system, they favor allowing banks to take equity positions in corporations, changing IRS regulations to encourage institutional investors to hold their positions in companies patiently, and limiting hostile takeovers and leveraged buyouts.

Because they see government regulatory agencies as both inefficient and adversarial, they argue that people with business experience should staff them. To make government even more business's partner, they advocate the creation of an American-style equivalent of Japan's MITI and the prompt rebuilding of our nation's decayed infrastructure. If all this requires a formal national industrial policy, then so be it. At a minimum, to make the United States competitive in world markets requires federal tax credits for retraining, reinvestment, and R & D; relaxation of antitrust laws to allow high-tech firms to pool technology and markets; increased government funding for engineering and science education; and technical and marketing support for exporting companies.

Many Corporatists would go further and target leading-edge industries for special government support. They would use the tax system to promote investment in those fields, allowing targeted industries to deduct more quickly the costs of their plants and equipment, and offering them cheap financing (perhaps through the Import-Export Bank). These Corporatists would use the power of government contracting to help defense industries make the transition to producing the commercial export technologies of tomorrow.

For most of this century, Corporatist values have been dominant in the Western world. As Newton demonstrated, though, for every force there is an equal and countervailing force. Beginning in the 1960s, the "green" reaction to Corporatism has been concerned with the quality of life.

≣ Community

In making our way three-quarters around the compass, we have identified many differences among three philosophies of political economy. We have also identified one important area of consensus: Libertarians, Egalitarians, and Corporatists all agree that economic efficiency is necessary, either as the means to the attainment of higher ends, or as an end in itself. Moreover, they agree that the pursuit of efficiency has social consequences, which they all find usually worth paying. In the eyes of others, those costs tend to involve—some would say, inherently require—trade-offs that are excessive, even malignant: a pact with the devil. To these Communitarians, Hamilton's embrace of the industrial revolution illustrates three Faustian exchanges.

A trade-off of the dignity
of human labor for efficiency

When Adam Smith advocated the further and continuing division of work tasks in order to improve manufacturing efficiency, he nonetheless conceded that

> in the progress of the division of labor, the employment of the far greater part of those who live by labor . . . comes to be con-

fined to a very few simple operations, frequently one or two.
. . . The man whose whole life is spent in performing a few
simple operations . . . has no occasion to exert his understanding or to exercise his invention. . . . He naturally loses,
therefore, the habit of such exertion, and generally becomes as
stupid and ignorant as it is possible for a human creature to
become.

A trade-off of the sense of community for efficiency

Tocqueville argued that industrialism was inevitable because,
as democracy spreads, "the demand for manufactured com-
modities becomes more general and extensive." He warned,
though, that the very social equality that was generating increased demand for manufactured goods would be undercut by
the system that provided them. Industrialization would destroy
the unique American condition of rural equality by creating
"an aristocracy of manufacturers." He suggested that early
nineteenth-century America was introducing invidious Euro-
pean-style social stratification in what up to then had been a
class-free society. In a factory town, he wrote, there is "no real
bond" between the owner and the worker.

> These two men meet in the factory but know not each other
> elsewhere; and whilst they come into contact on one point, they
> stand very wide apart on all others. The manufacturer asks noth-
> ing of the workman but his labor; the workman expects nothing
> from him but wages. The one contracts no obligation to protect,
> nor the other to defend; and they are not permanently connected
> either by habit or duty.

A trade-off of a clean and healthy environment for efficiency

Jefferson eventually conceded the need for manufacturing
to free America from its dependence on European military

powers, but he refused to accept the proposition that abandoning the high quality of rural life for the teeming, smoky, urban industrial arena was a net gain. "The mobs of great cities add just so much to the support of pure government as sores do to the strength of the human body."

To many individuals, such exchanges of quality of life for a high standard of living are morally unacceptable. They also see such practices as bad management in the long term, a squandering of human and natural resources. In the last two dozen years, most of these dissenters from the prevailing religion of economic progress have been called environmentalists. However, their value system (as we find below), which seems so contemporary, actually is rooted deeply in the humanistic, naturalistic belief that all humankind consists of a community—the human family—which is spread over the entire globe. For that reason, these individuals recently have taken to calling themselves Communitarians.

The origins of Communitarianism can be traced to Aristotle. (O'Toole's Rule: Whenever about to congratulate oneself on having an original idea, before going public remind yourself that the odds are Aristotle had it first!) Aristotle is particularly clear on questions of fundamental values, as he is on the related differences between ends and means. The end we should all aim for is "the good life," the use of our highest human faculties. His logic is simple: Everything should aim to fulfill its highest potential. Animals are stronger than people, ergo animals should do physical labor. Since only humans can reason, the proper end for humans is to use fully the capacity that distinguishes them from beasts. Therefore, the good life consists of intellectual and political activity—that which beasts cannot do. Since society is composed of reasoning humans, the "state exists for the sake of the good life." Those who participate in the activities that constitute the good life are the citizens of the polis. In the polis, justice consists of actions for "the common advantage," that is, for the good of others, and injustice consists of actions that despoil the sense of community, that do harm to others. "Justice, alone of the virtues, is thought to be 'another's good,' because it is related to our neighbors." Here we find the germ of modern Communitarianism, the humanistic valuing of the shared good life.

Unfortunately, say today's Communitarians, Aristotle had a bit more to say on the subject of the collective quality of life. When discussing exactly who constituted the community— who should enjoy the good life—he cautioned, "we ought not to include everybody." Those "included out" were more numerous than those included in! Among the outs were women, artisans, slaves, and foreigners, the latter category encompassing even native-born Athenians whose *grandparents* were aliens. Thus are modern Communitarians disappointed by the old master. They point to him, though, to show how the concept of community has expanded over time and must continue to expand further in the future; for example, Jefferson's concept wasn't much more inclusive than Aristotle's, but it was a small step in the right direction.

Traditionally, Communitarians have meant two things when they say community: first, the Jeffersonian face-to-face community of neighbors; second, the broader world community, the human family. Like Egalitarians, they have argued that Aristotle overstated the importance of the differences among humankind, much as he understated the importance of the common humanity that unites the species. On the other hand, today a strain of radical Communitarianism emphasizes the differences among the world's many diverse ethnic and racial *communities*, each with its own inviolable and unique culture. Tension between these opposing Communitarian views—between those who stress the *pluribus* and those who stress the *unum* as the chief value of American society— constitutes a major controversy inside academia today. On a more violent stage, the issue currently is being played out in the ethnic conflicts of Eastern Europe.

Aristotle built his notion of community from the ground up, as it were, based on his observations of nature. Like Locke and Rousseau, he believed that the family is the natural building block of the community. Families are "instinctive" to Aristotle—"like swarms of bees"—while to Rousseau they are held together by necessity. Either way, to Locke the family "draws with it mutual support and assistance, and a communion of interests, too." In the minds of all three philosophers, the "natural" progression is family ——> village ——> state, all of which are bound together by "a communion of interests." Not only common interests but, perhaps, common responsibilities as well. Wrote Locke:

> Everyone, as he is bound to preserve himself, and not quit his station willfully, so, by the like reason, when his own preservation comes not in competition, ought he, as much as he can, to preserve the rest of mankind, and not, unless it be to do justice to an offender, take away or impair the life, or what tends to be the preservation of the life, the liberty, health, limb or goods of another.

Here Locke goes at least as far as Mill would, five generations later, in asserting the human responsibility not to harm others. In addition, there is here and in his other writings a hint of Locke-the-Communitarian. This is ironic because Locke has long been the bête noire of environmentalists for advancing private claims to "the commons." After all, Locke said, "Whatsoever then he removes out of the state that nature has provided and left it in, he has mixed his labor with, and joined to it something that is his own, and thereby makes it his property." Locke also said, though, that no one could take more from nature than he could personally use, "at least where there is enough . . . left in common for others." This statement of responsibility for conservation to benefit future generations seems every bit as strong, ecologically speaking, as John Rawls's modern "just savings principle," which claims that it is unjust for Egalitarians to engage in acts of redistribution that beggar the future.

In essence, for Communitarians the key issue is to distinguish what is rightly mine from what is rightly ours. Of course, in the state of nature, the Communitarians' particular base of reference, everything is ours. That is why Communitarians' critics often accuse them of being utopians, of irrationally longing to return to the state of nature, the Garden of Eden where all was pristine and fecund. As Rousseau depicted it, this was the Golden Age in which "the produce of the earth furnished [mankind] with all he needed, and instinct told him how to use it," and "singing and dancing, the true offspring of love and leisure, became the amusement, or rather the occupation of men and women assembled together with nothing else to do."

This was the age when, in Locke's phrase, "All the world was America": undeveloped, uncivilized, unspoiled, and unpopulated. (To Locke and his contemporaries, the extensive Native civilization was invisible.) At any rate, this Eden was lost, according to Rousseau, "when property was introduced." This development was "some fatal accident, which, for the public good, should never have happened." Rousseau saw this fatal accident as somewhat analogous to the Biblical Fall, since along with private property the afflictions of necessity were introduced: some people gained property, and others were forced to labor for them. Labor, after all, is Adam's Curse ("Cursed is the ground for thy sake; in toil shalt thou eat of it all the days of thy life"), and toil and drudgery is the curse for *those* men and women who do not own property. Thus, the fatal accident—the leaving of nature—introduces a distinction between the classes, an eternal division of the once-united community between those who toil and those who don't (or, in Marxist terms, between labor and capital).

Of course, to non-Marxists like Locke, those who don't "labor" can still be said to "work" when they invest their capital. Aristotle had been trying to get at a related point when he made a distinction between good work and bad work. Bad work is labor, manual work that should only be done by beasts, slaves, machines, or women. In contrast, good work is closer to leisure; it is mental work that only can be done by people who are free of the need to toil. Bad work, then, is instrumental, in that it extrinsically supports *others'* leisure to engage in good work, while the latter is an end in itself and provides intrinsic rewards to those who engage in it. Marxists ask for an equal distribution of property to end the manifest injustice of this two-class system; Communitarians have a different idea.

Communitarians ask, is it not possible to design all work in such a way that it is intrinsically rewarding for all those who do it? Aristotle thought he had the answer to that question: automation. In the fourth century B.C., he posited that if ever it became possible that "the shuttle would weave and the plectrum touch the lyre without a hand to guide them, chief workmen would not want servants, nor masters slaves." Only automation could free all men and women from the tyranny of necessity, and all could then participate in good work. In this prescient passage we find the seeds of a modern paradox: machine progress, the bane of Communitarians, is at once the cause of the problem they identify and its solution. Indeed, modern technologists tell us that it is necessary to go through the enslaving stage of "dark satanic mills" to get to the age of the labor-saving robot. In 1930, Keynes addressed Aristotle's question and predicted that, in a mere five generations, automation finally would have freed all of humankind from the dictates of necessity. Unhappily, until then, Keynes said we would have to continue playing by the economists' basic principle that necessity requires self-interested, dog-eat-dog competition. "For at least another hundred years we must pretend to ourselves and to every one that fair is foul and foul is fair; for foul is useful and fair is not. Avarice and usury and precaution must be our gods for a little longer still. For only they can lead us out of the tunnel of economic necessity into daylight."

Keynes sounds a bit like Aristotle in his tolerance of injustice while waiting for the deus ex machina of abundance. To the ancient, though, Keynes's admonition might smack of moral confusion of the ends and means. To Aristotle, some of the mental work undertaken by Keynes-the-scholar, who was a successful stock market speculator on the side, might not have qualified as good work. To Aristotle, wealth should not be accumulated endlessly for its own sake, but merely to provide the means to support the good life. To the extent that Keynes-the-speculator invested in order to support his research and writing, Aristotle would have approved; had Keynes speculated in order to engage in conspicuous consumption, Aristotle would have condemned him.

Marx, on the other hand, would have denounced Keynes as a "parasite." Marx might have conceded that financiers like Keynes can be said to increase the overall wealth of the nation by putting their capital to productive use, but he thought that in so doing they degrade the unity of society. To Marx, the increase in the wealth of the few reduces the dignity of the many who are forced to labor to support them. Worse, the worker becomes a mere cog in an industrial machine that "converts the laborer into a crippled monstrosity, by forcing his detailed dexterity at the expense of productive capabilities and instincts." Echoing Smith, Marx not only says that craftsmanship has been replaced by the dull rote of industrial work but, worse, workers have no leisure time in which to recreate themselves. They become like Aristotelian machines or slaves— wage slaves—while the owner/capitalist extracts the surplus value and enjoys the leisure. Marx's description of a two-class society is remarkably like Aristotle's, except that Marx stresses the injustice inherent in the plight of the have-nots, whereas Aristotle extols the good life of the haves. While Marx would agree with Aristotle (and Keynes) on what the good life

entails, it bothered him morally that the wage slave is denied
the freedom, education, and wherewithal to be a participating
member in Aristotle's polis: the community.

Here we must make an important distinction. Because
Marxists are concerned primarily with achieving a high standard of living for all, they focus on the necessity of a just
distribution of property; Communitarians, concerned primarily with achieving a high quality of life for all, focus on the
necessity of a just distribution of good work. Revelations from
eastern Europe have recently shown what this difference might
mean in practice: there, the former communist rulers could
act as if justice had been served fully when factories were
owned collectively, even if the working conditions in them
were Dickensian, and they spewed tons of pollution into the
environment. Communitarians do not believe that state ownership of the means of production, in and of itself, will address
quality-of-life issues, so for three generations they have sought
to improve the quality of life in workplaces regardless of who
owns them. In the early part of this century, the American
Thorstein Veblen called for greater attention to the common
"instinct of workmanship" and greater sensitivity to the inherent human "taste for effective work." He believed that all men
and women have a strong desire for a sense of mastery, self-
esteem, and competence in their individual work. This Communitarian concern was pursued in earnest by a subsequent
generation of workplace humanists, including Abraham Maslow and Douglas McGregor.

Contemporary workplace humanism stems from the efforts
of the early nineteenth-century industrialist Robert Owen, who
created a model business in his textile factory in New Lanark,
Scotland and was the first to introduce relatively short working
hours, a grievance procedure, and guaranteed employment
during times of economic downturn. He invented contributory
health, disability, and retirement plans and provided clean,
decent housing for his workers and their families. Most singu-

larly, he took young children out of his factory and put them in a school that was the first to stress learning as a pleasurable experience. He is also credited with having established both the consumer and producer cooperative movements. He argued that choices made by society, not laws of the market, determined social conditions. For his efforts, Marx and Engels singled him out for special scorn and condemnation in the *Communist Manifesto*.

In the final analysis, Communitarians differ from Marxists in their humanistic, as opposed to economic, orientation. They put men and women—dignified, rational, altruistic humans—at the center of the universe. They believe that the peculiarly human qualities of reasoning and speech not only grant Natural Rights to every individual but unite the entire species in a greater commonwealth. Mill made this Communitarian point most strongly when he said that humankind is different from other animals

> first, in being capable of sympathising, not solely with their offspring, or, like some of the more noble animals, with some superior animal who is kind to them, but with all human and even with all sentient beings. Secondly, in having a more developed intelligence, which gives a wider range to the whole of their sentiments, whether self-regarding or sympathetic. By virtue of their superior intelligence, even apart from his superior range of sympathy, a human being is capable of apprehending a community of interest between himself and the human society of which he forms a part.

Communitarians thus differ greatly from Libertarians, Egalitarians, and Corporatists in their belief that humans are not only sympathetic but capable of altruism on behalf of their fellows. For this, Communitarians are called idealistic, and said to fail to understand that human nature is, at base, self-interested. (Mill answered the charge in this way: "The deep-rooted selfishness which forms the general character of the existing state of society, is so deeply rooted, only because the whole course of existing institutions tends to foster it.") Libertarians, in particular, score Communitarians for a willingness to sacrifice individuality to obtain the collective good. But when Mill speaks of community, he does not mean sameness. Among the moral philosophers Mill was the most concerned with the repressive effects of society, "the tyranny of custom" that crushes individuality. He recognized (before Mao proved the point) that uniformity does not enhance the quality of life.

A major distinction between Libertarianism and Communitarianism is this: liberty has to do with *independence,* community with *interdependence.* Another way of seeing the difference: Libertarians stress individual rights, Communitarians stress common responsibilities. Mill, who had so much to say about the necessity of rights in preserving individual liberty, also saw that rampant individualism would undermine the very sense of community that separates us from the beasts. He thus stressed the issue of balance between individual rights and community responsibilities. For instance, he believed that the right of a British subject to a trial by jury was balanced by a concomitant responsibility to serve on a jury. Citizens have numerous responsibilities: to pay taxes, educate their children, serve in the army, and provide "other joint work necessary to the interest of society." On the Communitarian issue of responsibility he went much further than any other writer (at least, further than any other Communitarian who was also a Libertarian!). In fact, he would require much more of citizens than is required in America today, arguing that citizens should "perform certain acts of individual beneficence, such as saving a fellow creature's life or imposing to protect the defenseless against ill-usage—things which whenever it is obviously a man's duty to do he may rightfully be made responsible to society for not doing."

The essential sources of community, then, come close to what Christians mean by charity, what humanistic psychologists mean by empathy, what the French revolutionaries meant by *fraternité*, and what the Japanese mean by *amae*. The effect of this interdependence and compassion was best described by Aristotle: "When men are friends, they have no need of justice."

Locke had similarly characterized natural society as "men living together according to reason without a common superior on earth, with authority to judge between them." Of course, humankind then went and altered nature, and thus lost that common bond of fraternity. The solution to Rousseau was clear: he advocated a return to the state of nature, calling on humankind to divest itself of the artifices of civilization, "renouncing its advances, in order to renounce its vices." Marx partially agreed: he thought it impossible to go back to a lost historical era, but felt it necessary to move through industrialism to the next, higher stage of civilization where humans would gain a new, advanced sense of community. Of course, much of what Marx had to say on this subject was as naive and impractical as Rousseau, but Marx was the first to understand that economic progress has vast social implications. Where Corporatists saw the industrial revolution as merely a shift in the mechanical modes of production, Marx called attention to such consequent changes as the destruction of entire social classes, the altering of relations among nations, and even demographic transformations (and, if he failed to call attention directly to the problems of environmental degradation, he noted the effects of factory life on the mortality and morbidity of urban workers). In short, Rousseau, Locke, and Marx all emphasized that human actions altered nature, and not necessarily for the better.

Environmentalism

All the great philosophers saw humankind as *a part* of nature, yet somehow *apart* from it as well, by virtue of the intellectual superiority of the race. Darwin first placed humans squarely *in* nature, calling attention to our anatomical, physiological, and behavioral commonalities with other animals. This new perspective led, in subsequent generations, to a refocusing of Communitarianism. For if we are a part of nature, does this not mean that we despoil ourselves when we despoil nature? Significantly, this connection had first been made not by Westerners but by Asians and such indigenous peoples as Native Americans.

Nearly a hundred years after Darwin, Westerners finally made the ecological connection between human behavior and the natural environment. In 1962, Rachel Carson brought the issue of environmental responsibility to light in her book *Silent Spring*.

> The history of the earth has been a history of interaction between living things and their surroundings. To a large extent, the physical form and the habits of the earth's vegetation and its animal life have been molded by the environment. Considering the whole span of earthly time, the opposite effect, in which life actually modifies its surroundings, has been relatively slight. Only within the moment of time represented by the present century has one species—man—acquired significant power to alter the nature of his world.

Communitarians combine the two intellectual threads— humans apart from nature and humans a part of nature—in the notion of trusteeship, or social responsibility, and they combine the issues of human community and community with nature in the concept of the quality of life. Economic and industrial practices, they point out, affect both, revealing the illogic of Aristotle's limited view of community. Environmental problems know no boundaries of social class or national origin. They are thus problems we all have in common. We are united, finally, say the environmentalists, on spaceship earth. Again, we find the seeds of this new idea in the writings of the ancients. Building on Aristotle's continuum of family ——→ village ——→ state, Marcus Aurelius, writing c. 150 B.C., took the next logical step in the progression: ——→ globe.

> If our intellectual part is common, the reason also, in respect of which we are rational human beings, is common; if this is so, common also is the reason which commands us what to do, and what not to do; if this is so, there is a common law also; if this is so, we are fellow citizens; if this is so, we are members of the same political community; if this is so, the world is in a manner a state.

To Aristotle, the family is a "domestic community" and a state is a "political community." Both are communities in that they are composed of individuals associated for a common purpose. Logically, then, a global community must have a common purpose. To the environmentalist/humanist, that purpose is the protection of the biosphere—the insuring of its safety so that all who are born in the future can lead Aristotle's good life. Since the protection of the environment requires cooperation among nations, truly *united nations,* the modern Communitarian echoes Epictetus, who had written, some fifty years before Aurelius, "There is but one course open to men, to do as Socrates did: never to reply to one who asks his country, 'I am an Athenian' or 'I am a Corinthian,' but 'I am a citizen of the universe'."

Communitarians thus part company with Libertarians, Egalitarians, and Corporatists on yet another significant issue: their philosophy does not assume the sovereignty of the nation state. Like Aristotle, Communitarians start with family obligations, but they move quickly to duties owed neighbors and, most singularly, to strangers. These strangers include not only people from other communities and other races and religions, but people beyond the borders of one's own nation. With considerable effort, traditional Libertarianism, Egalitarianism, and Corporatism can be interpreted to encompass such a broad perspective, but Communitarianism differs from the other philosophies in that it is predicated on the assumption of globalism.

In this regard, as in its rejection of the narrow, economic concept of efficiency, Communitarianism departs radically from the other belief systems we have examined. Moreover, unlike the other philosophies, which are concerned solely with creating healthy socioeconomic environments, Communitarianism is equally concerned with creating a healthy physical environment. Communitarianism also stresses the responsibilities of current generations to future generations far more than do the other three value sets.

In light of these many differences, it might be concluded that the pursuit of community is not comparable with the pursuit of liberty, equality, and efficiency. That would be to ignore the many overlaps and complementarities between community and the three other values. For instance, Communitarians often line up with Egalitarians on matters of Natural Rights and social equality, and with Libertarians on matters of civil liberties, traditional family values, entrepreneurialism, decentralized decisionmaking, and voluntary associations. On many other important matters, the differences between community and the adjoining values to the north and south of it on the compass are matters more of degree than kind: Libertarians stress competition and Communitarians stress cooperation, and Egalitarians stress rights and Communitarians stress responsibilities, but these are not either/or distinctions; more precisely, they are differences of emphasis that blur at the edges.

Remarkably, there is also a blurring between the desires of those who pursue efficiency and those who pursue community. Although these values occupy opposite poles on our compass, places where they come together do exist (much as we discovered with the opposition of liberty to equality). A close rereading of *The Republic* illustrates the point. Our earlier Corporatist interpretation of Plato's ideal state could be complemented with a Communitarian interpretation almost as convincing. Plato's desire for efficiency and effectiveness is matched, to nearly an equal degree, by his desire for social coordination and harmony. Indeed, he attempts to bring these two poles together by defining the good society as an efficient and harmonious whole.

While Plato does not completely succeed in this attempt to fuse efficiency and community—and no Westerner has ever succeeded in doing so—the reconciliation of these apparent opposites is comparatively effortless in Asian cultures. In examining the rise of the successful business culture in East Asia after World War II, Tu Wei-ming notes that the Confucian perspective marries efficiency and community. One might say that contemporary Japan almost does the trick, though it is slightly out of balance on the efficiency side, as Akio Morita notes (and completely out of kilter when it comes to accepting duties to those outside its borders).

In contrast, American history has been played out largely on the liberty/equality axis. The tensions between these two values have been so profound that it is often difficult for Americans to accept that our history is unique in this regard. Before the Enlightenment in the West (and for the rest of the world, after that time as well) social, political, and economic history was enacted mainly along the community/efficiency axis. The prime concern of all preliterate societies was to achieve sufficient social harmony to mount an effective collective front in the battle against nature. Preliterate peoples were all communities, whose function was to provide the cohesion required for the groups' survival. The Western emphasis on the individual caused this focus to be lost. While the West won the war against nature by means of modern science and technology, in contrast, Asians gradually accepted modern science without losing as much of traditional community values.

Again, this distinction is a matter of degree and emphasis.

The tension between efficiency and community never fully disappeared in the West—witness again the struggle between Hamilton and Jefferson. Nonetheless, the emphasis in the West for the last two hundred years has been on the tension between liberty and equality, with both capitalists and communists agreed on the value of efficiency. Now, due to a concatenation of developments—the worldwide population explosion, periodic resource crises, the collapse of communism, to cite just three—concerns along the community/efficiency axis have surfaced with a force that surprises Westerners. We are surprised because we had been preoccupied for two centuries with an entirely different agenda.

Contemporary Communitarianism

Historically, many Americans believed that the pursuit of the ends of liberty and efficiency would lead to the good society, and that the means to those ends was the effective application of technology. But when Communitarians examine what, in fact, technology has wrought they see a degraded and abused physical and social environment. A contemporary Communitarian, Neil Postman, argues, "The uncontrolled growth of technology destroys the vital sources of our humanity. It creates a culture without a moral foundation. It undermines certain mental processes and social relations that make human life worth living." The culprit is the Corporatist belief that "the primary, if not the only, goal of human labor and thought is efficiency."

The second culprit is the Libertarian assumption of *homo economicus*—Adam Smith's belief that the good society depends on humankind's "propensity to barter, truck and exchange one thing for another." This premise was challenged in the broadest expression of modern Communitarianism, E. F. Schumacher's 1973 book *Small is Beautiful*, the subtitle of which is quintessentially Communitarian: "Economics as if

People Mattered." Schumacher advocated policies to conserve natural resources, end pollution, and create opportunities for "good work" for all the citizens of the globe. To this end, he called for greater social control of industry—though not necessarily state control, which he feared would lead to bureaucratization inimical to the quality of life. Schumacher's fundamental assumption was that humans are the measure of all things, thus traditional economic measures, in fact, lead to *inefficiency*. He illustrated the difference between economic inefficiency and what he called social inefficiency: An unregulated market creates social inefficiencies because it does not produce enough public goods (for example, public transportation); it is short-term oriented; it produces "externalities" such as pollution; and it treats people as things. (To the economist, land, labor, and capital are fungible; the environmentalist/ humanist treats all three differently, because some land is a renewable resource, other land is nonrenewable, and humans are never to be treated as means).

Communitarians of Schumacher's persuasion believe that economic growth as traditionally defined is not necessary and, in fact, is often undesirable because we live in a world of finite resources. Concomitantly, progress does not necessarily result from the introduction of advanced technology, which may have untoward consequences for the environment and for the people who work with it and near it. Hence, Communitarian rules of thumb include: small is better than big, decentralized better than centralized, local better than national, participation better than diktat, demassified better than standardized, and community-centered activities better than self-interested ones. There is thus a paradox in what they believe and advocate; since the world is one, and all humans are of the same species, they say we must learn to "think globally, act locally."

Communitarians criticize modern society for wasting such nonrenewable resources as fossil fuels; for overpopulating and polluting the globe (for example, the destruction of the rain forests); and for engaging in conspicuous consumption that adds nothing to the quality of life (our materialistic civilization breeds alienation, rootlessness, and wantonness, as manifested by crime, violence, drug abuse, and the pursuit of instant gratification). Similarly, many corporations produce shoddy, unnecessary goods while leaving basic human needs unmet. Finally, a worldwide sense of community is lost as governments pursue "them versus us" policies that end up, self-defeatingly, harming all of humankind. (The current "politically correct" position is slightly different: because "unity is the completed puzzle, and diversity the pieces," it is incumbent on governments to stress the virtues and contributions of each ethnic and racial community.)

The Communitarian agenda follows from these criticisms. They call for social planning for land and resource use, a limit of economic growth to "sustainable levels," and the establishment of decentralized offices of technology assessment and environmental impact, to be coordinated internationally. They favor industrial practices that preserve biological diversity and prevent climate change. Starting locally, they wish to create an ethic of voluntary public service and an ethic of conservation. Within workplaces, they seek to establish employee ownership as part of overall quality of worklife programs. Internationally, they support an invigorated North/South dialogue channeled through such global agencies as WHO and UNESCO, and in particular, increased emphasis on "sustainable" economic development in the Third World.

In 1991 Communitarianism was formalized as a movement in America with the publication of "The Responsive Communitarian Platform," a Tocquevillian call for the reinvigoration of families, neighborhoods, and such secondary institutions as professional, social, religious, and ethnic voluntary associations. Since such organizations stress responsibilities, duties, sharing, and serving others, the Communitarians see them as effective counterbalances to the prevailing American ethic of private self-interest. The Communitarian platform also called for the rewriting of divorce laws to insure child support, the alteration of workplaces to make them more family oriented, national and local service for youth, and strict limits on gun ownership.

Now that we have made our way 360 degrees around the compass, we note one more significant characteristic of its polar nature. On the north/south axis, Liberty and Equality are basically Western values that emerged during the Enlightenment. These values are concerned with matters of individual rights. On the east/west axis, Community and Efficiency are more universal values, with roots in both Western and Eastern thought that reach back nearly three thousand years. These two values are concerned with societal goods that are shared in common.

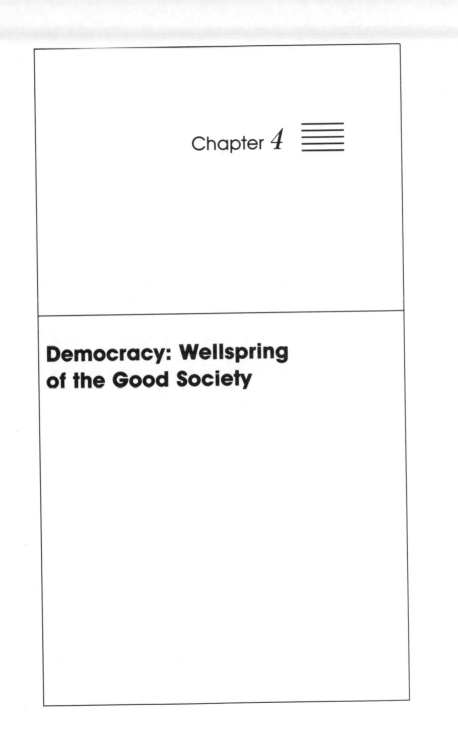

Chapter *4* ≣

Democracy: Wellspring
of the Good Society

Such ideas [liberty and equality, for example] are the substance of ethics. Ethical thought consists of the systematic examination of the relations of human beings to each other, the conceptions, interests and ideals from which human ways of treating one another spring, and the systems of value on which such ends of life are based. These beliefs about how life should be lived, what men and women should be and do, are objects of moral inquiry; and when applied to groups and nations, and, indeed, mankind as a whole, are called political philosophy, which is but ethics applied to society.

—ISAIAH BERLIN

The four ideas we have examined—liberty, equality, efficiency and community—are the polar forces tugging at all modern polities. Indeed, the tensions among those values have provided the drama to political life in the West since the time of Hobbes. In particular, the choice between liberty and equality is said to be the most fundamental, and inescapable, of all the trade-offs facing society. During this century, Marxist Egalitarianism's manifest disdain for civil liberties has provided tragic empirical support for the commonly held premise that these two primary values are incompatible. Thus, in the writings of contemporary political economists and political philosophers, liberty and equality are often presented as polar alternatives:

Liberty

vs.

Equality

The liberty versus equality trade-off is not the only difficult dilemma facing modern societies. Since the dawn of the industrial era, as the world has become increasingly complex, the choices faced by society have become concomitantly intricate. Some, like Hamilton, for the sake of economic growth and technological advance, have been willing to sacrifice other valued ends. Others, like Jefferson, have been concerned primarily with Communitarian values such as the quality of life, and have been just as willing to compromise other ends. In recent decades, economists have documented the consequences of pursuing both the Jeffersonian and Hamiltonian alternatives. Economists say that for every increment of environmental quality a society gains, a measure of efficiency is lost (as when a scrubber is placed on an industrial smokestack, or when any environmental, consumer, health, or safety regulation is enforced). The opposite is said to be true, as well: gains in efficiency from power plants endanger the quality of life of host communities. In the modern industrial state, then, there is a constant, nagging tension between Corporatist and Communitarian values:

Community ◄——— *vs.* ———► Efficiency

Another domain of painful choice emerges whenever a modern society attempts to close the income gap between its haves and have-nots. Economists argue that highly progressive rates of taxation reduce incentives to work, welfare transfer payments create bureaucratic waste, that motivation is lost when financial rewards are separated from productive contribution, and entrepreneurial effort diminishes when the size of jackpots from capital gains gets too small. In such instances, society is faced with Arthur Okun's great trade-off between equality and efficiency:

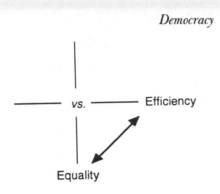

As environmentalism has become of increasing concern in recent years, a new tradeoff has developed between the goals of conservationists and the needs of their occasional allies, the labor unions. Two examples: The prohibition of timber cutting to save virgin forests, and the closing of irremediably polluting industrial plants, have led to the loss of blue-collar jobs in America and Europe. Outside the capitalist West, the resultant drabness of life in those Marxist countries most dedicated to Egalitarian policies illustrates another kind of trade-off between the quality of life and equality. Today, all around the world, Egalitarian and Communitarian values are in tension, in one way or another:

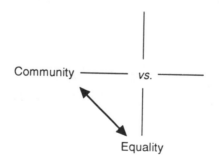

Mill, as we have seen, called attention to the many trade-offs between individual desires and the collective good; bans on smoking in public and driving a hundred miles per hour, and zoning laws that prohibit such entrepreneurial activity as the freedom to build and operate mini-malls in residential neighborhoods, are instances of society's infringements on personal freedom in the name of the common good. Thus, trade-offs also exist between Libertarian and Communitarian values:

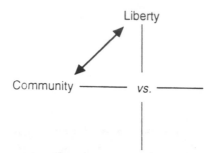

Moving completely around the quadrant, we come finally to the trade-offs Americans have been most willing to make, or most willing to deny exist! Taxation to support the military, and regulations promulgated by the Securities and Exchange Commission and the Federal Communications Commission, are examples of infringements on personal liberty that are justified for purpose of efficiency. Hence, there are also trade-offs between Libertarian and Corporatist values:

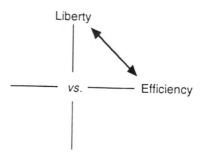

In sum, the quadrant can illustrate most of the salient political and economic issues debated today in the capitals of the developed world in terms of trade-offs among those with differing values, objectives—or dreams. These differing values—in effect, differing concepts of the good society—revolve around the very ideas debated for centuries by the great moral and political philosophers. This discovery illuminates the relevance of these writings to modern issues, but it doesn't yet answer the central question of our enquiry: Can the good society be created in a world of conflicting values?

≣ The Power of Balance

We began our enquiry with the broadly accepted proposition, *the fundamental task of every legitimate government is to secure the good society for its citizenry.* We soon found that each philosopher who advanced this notion also offered a different definition of such a society. We then discovered that current political conflicts reflect our own differing views of the good society, each view rooted in our personal dreams or values. In order to define the good society, we must now address the penultimate question: Whose values are right?

The reader who has followed the argument to this point will doubtless have anticipated my conclusion: *Objectively, none of the values of liberty, equality, efficiency, or community can be demonstrated to be better than the others.* Values are, after all, matters of individual preference and, like questions of taste, are never to be disputed. This conclusion may give the appearance of begging the issue, but I suggest that it does exactly the opposite. If all four values are good, then it is incumbent on every government dedicated to the welfare of its citizenry to treat all four value sets (and their many permutations) as legitimate objectives. Reconciling tensions between these values is a matter of political process. All that can be said in describing the good society is that those governments who perform the process to the greatest satisfaction of their citizens are to be preferred to those in which the reconciliation is arbitrary, hence to the least satisfaction of the citizenry. We call the former societies just because they respond evenhandedly to the conflicting needs and desires of all their citizens.

One process is peculiarly capable of achieving reconciliation among these conflicting values: *democracy*. The genius of a well-functioning democracy is to be responsive to all of a nation's citizens, constituencies, and interest groups and to serve as a process for balancing their conflicting demands. In short, a democracy attempts to satisfy all competing interests. In doing so, it not only serves the ends of justice, it establishes its own legitimacy. Precision requires at least two clarifications of these assertions. First, there is no warrant that democracy invariably leads to the good society. Democracy is inherently an imperfect process, and the good society is no fixed thing. Second, the good society should not be viewed as a wishy-washy compromise represented by a single point at the very center of the quadrant:

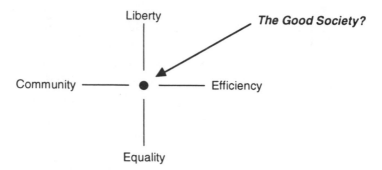

Such a point represents a variety of justice, but it is an extremely circumscribed one. The alternative is predicated on the assumption that, since liberty, equality, efficiency, and community are all good things, a well-functioning democracy would tend toward creating policies that provide as much of all four values as possible. Evidence of the citizenry's nearly boundless desire for all these values is found in the fact that few ideologues would be satisfied, as Marx was, with absolute equality at the cost of all other objectives, or would want one hundred percent of liberty, as Sumner was at the expense of everything else. Most modern men and women want as much liberty, as much equality, as much efficiency, and as much community as they can reasonably get. How, or even whether, this condition can be achieved is an important question to which we will return, but ideally the full domain of the good society might be illustrated this way:

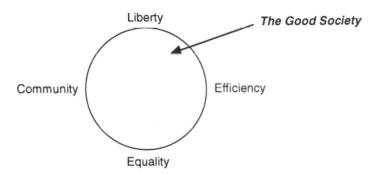

Of course, no democracy has realized this potential (the ideal, by definition, is unattainable). In practice, each decision democratically made, each law passed, and each regulation formulated favors one value over the others—but *not the same value every time*. Consequently, the various constituencies of a democracy find themselves alternatively pleased and displeased by the policies that emanate from the system. Even when displeased, though, they should never grow so irrevocably disenchanted as to challenge its legitimacy. If the decisionmaking process is open and fair, democracy is thus a condition of continuing tension and periodic dissatisfaction. It is also the only condition that modern men and women accept as just. Reinhold Niebuhr put the case for democracy in this way: "Man's capacity for justice makes democracy possible; but man's inclination to injustice makes democracy necessary."

Here we must draw a crucial distinction: liberty, equality, efficiency, and community are goals, values, dreams, or objectives—ends, in the philosophical sense; democracy is a process—a means. Therefore, the problem of democracy has no ultimate solution—no optimal mix of programs, no final rest-

ing place on the quadrant that will produce a utopia perma-
nently acceptable to the entire citizenry. As long as people have
different values, and for as long as conditions of society are
susceptible to change, the realization of the good society
through democracy is, for now and forever, a dynamic process.
The resources of a nation must be constantly managed: expanded then gathered, gathered then distributed, each person
or group sometimes gaining, sometimes losing, but always
treated fairly and with respect. Above all, always heard. When
this process is working, even those who have the least success
in realizing their objectives will conclude that the system itself
is just. As Jesse Jackson maintained during the 1984 presidential race, "Democracy doesn't guarantee success, it only guarantees opportunity."

On these points, the philosophers offer three main principles of democratic justice worth noting.

Voice. According to Mill, "It is a personal injustice to
withhold from anyone, unless for the prevention of greater
evils, the ordinary privilege of having his voice reckoned in the
disposal of affairs in which he has the same interests as other
people."

Power. According to Montesquieu, true democracy exists
"when the body of the people is possessed of the supreme
power." (And Aristotle said that power must only be exercised
for "the common good.")

Respect. According to Kant, the rulers must treat the ruled
as ends rather than means. Moreover, in a democracy, the ruler
is equal to the ruled, and no better.

When a democratic system works according to these principles, it can be said to be just and thus apt to lead to the good
society. Hence, the process of democracy is, at its core, aimed
at the creation of "moral symmetry" between the competing
values of men and women of equal voice, power and respect.
To use George Will's phrase, the process tends toward "an
equilibrium based on justice."

≡ Why Extreme Positions Are Unjust

This equilibrium would be radically upset if the nation were to pursue one or the other of the various extreme courses advocated by Libertarians, Egalitarians, Corporatists, and Communitarians. The adoption of laissez faire would be anathema to those who seek greater social equality and security, to those who seek protection for consumers and desire clean air and water, and to those who wish to build the national infrastructure needed for global competitiveness. Similarly, undiluted Egalitarian programs would create unacceptable consequences in the eyes of Libertarians, Corporatists, and Communitarians: decreased incentives for performance, increased bureaucracy, and an overall decline in both the standard of living and quality of life. Extreme Corporatist solutions, too, would fail in the United States to generate support at the other three poles because what most Americans fear more than the power of big government or big business or big labor is the possibility of these three combining their power in unholy consort. Finally, many Communitarian policies to enhance the quality of life would be rejected by their opponents as elitist, that is, serving only the interests of a minority wealthy enough to be unconcerned with improving their own material standard of living (or insensitive to the others' desires for material progress). Thus, policies put forward by members of each extreme ideological camp will fail because they are primarily either/or propositions that exclude, or at least subordinate, the interests of all other factions. In essence, extreme solutions are seen as *unjust*, because they do violence to the legitimate values of the majority.

Significantly, that majority is not a monolith; if it were, it could tyrannically impose its will on a permanent minority. Instead, the majority is made up of a shifting number of factions, and that is the genius of what is called pluralism. In his "Federalist Paper Number 10" James Madison put forward the radical proposition that complex modern democracies, unlike small preindustrial nations, would have no permanent minorities or majorities but would be comprised of changing and shifting composites based on a continuing process of compromise and conciliation. "The smaller the society, the fewer probably will be the distinct parties and interests composing it," he wrote, but "extend the sphere, and you take in a greater variety of parties and interests; you make it less probable that a majority of the whole will have a common motive to invade the rights of other citizens."

To modern pluralists like Sir Isaiah Berlin, Madison's system represents the ultimate safeguard against the imposition of a fascist, communist, or other extreme ideology. Berlin studies the totalitarian systems of this century and calls our attention to the fact that they were each based on one or another of the value systems we have examined. "It is as well to realise that these great movements began with ideas in people's heads; ideas about what relations between men have been, are, might be and should be; and to realise how they came to be transformed in the name of a vision of some supreme goal in the minds of leaders, above all of the prophets with armies at their backs."

While such movements start out as essentially moral in intent, they end up being immoral in practice when they impose themselves on those with differing views, needs, and beliefs. Berlin writes that Libertarianism and Egalitarianism are noble in conception, but immoral in practice. "Both liberty and equality are among the primary goals pursued by human beings through many centuries; but total liberty for wolves is death to the lambs." And total equality is poison for wolves. Democratic pluralism protects society's lambs and wolves from the tyrannical realization of each other's most noble dreams. This compromise is far better than the totalitarian alternative, yet Berlin admits that something about pluralism is intrinsically dissatisfying: both lambs and wolves have due process, but neither party will have its way. Democracy produces neither perfect liberty nor perfect equality, but dissatisfying (to some) amounts of both. This is "bad," of course, because both liberty and equality are "good"! In the Tocquevillian tradition of political philosophy, Berlin concludes that the "collisions of values" inherent in democracy are inevitable and tragic. "We are doomed to choose, and every choice may entail an irreparable loss."

This tradition of the tragic trade-off is compelling. Indeed, it forms the basis not only for modern political philosophy but for the discipline of economics. Indeed, practically all difficult decisions in any endeavor involve a weighing or balancing of values. Democracy, in particular, requires untold numbers of tradeoffs every day, most of them eminently sensible, and a fair number rather irritating. But can we call this inevitable collision of values "tragic"? Moreover, are the few truly tragic compromises absolutely necessary? In practice, the difficult choices in politics are not about how to do a good thing rather than a bad thing, as Berlin implies, but how to do a good thing without jeopardizing another good thing. Mortimer Adler offers an alternative to the Berlinian view: "When both liberty and equality are limited by the restraints of justice, they are not incompatible. The actual conflict is between libertarianism, which asks for unlimited liberty, and egalitarianism, which asks for complete equality. There is never a conflict between limited liberty and limited equality."

From this thought we can deduce a moral or ethical standard for justice in society: Extreme policies that make impossible the achievement of other legitimate objectives are immoral. Thus, the pursuit of liberty is moral, while the pursuit of radical Libertarianism is immoral when and if that pursuit denies others the realization of the values of equality, efficiency, and community. Adler, himself, suggests the following principle of justice:

No one should have more liberty than justice allows (that is, no more than individuals can use without injuring anyone else or the general welfare); and no society should establish more equality than justice requires . . . namely, that all are *haves* and none are *have nots* in that they are deprived of a decent livelihood. However, among the *haves*, some will *have more* and others *have less*, according to the degree to which they contribute to the economic welfare of society as a whole.

(We will soon examine several public policies consistent with Adler's principle—government programs that seem to support his contention that opposing social values, when tempered by justice, are not incompatible.)

Berlin's theory that democratic pluralism is the source of the good society, or as good a society as we are likely to get in this vale of tears, has at least two other shortcomings, according to some critics. First, pluralism can be said to lead to a kind of moral relativism in which all values are considered equal. At one level this criticism seems absurd: how can it be morally wrong for the democratic process to be value-neutral in the face of four good ends? No responsible critic doubts that the *system* should be morally neutral as to the four values, but some argue that society degenerates into collective cynicism when the *citizenry* no longer distinguishes between right and wrong ends or good policies and bad. Hence, a clarifying distinction must be drawn between the individuals in the system and the system itself. While individuals can maintain their passions for one or more of the competing values, the process must not favor one or more of these passions. Individuals may be Libertarians, Egalitarians, Corporatists, or Communitarians, but the system must be only democratic. That is, the system must maintain the arena in which competing values can contend fairly.

Furthermore, the critics fail to notice that democracy as a system is not value-neutral. In the words of Vaclav Havel, democracy depends on the citizenry sharing such values as "decency, reason, responsibility, sincerity, civility and toler-ance." In short, there needs to be a civic culture, with com-monly held values concerning the process of democracy. This is a far cry from the moral relativism of "do your own thing." As Madison wrote, "The latent causes of faction are . . . sown in the nature of man. Since the *causes* of faction cannot be removed . . . relief is sought in the means of controlling its *effects*." That means of control is not power but the social contract: our agreement to abide by the values of democratic pluralism.

The second frequent charge against pluralism, more prob-lematic, is that conflict-ridden pluralistic systems regress into stasis; immobilized by the forces of competing factions, they become unable to change in the face of a growing number of intractable problems. On this score, American democracy has recently been criticized as "a trap" in which the self-indulgent pursuit of individual interests precludes any sacrifice for the common good. The result is the gridlock or paralysis of Ameri-can democracy captured so brilliantly in the words of Jean François-Poncet, the former French Foreign Minister: "It is hard to take seriously that a nation has deep problems if they can be fixed with a 50 cent-a-gallon gasoline tax." His point is that America is so paralyzed by the selfish pursuit of self-interest that it cannot take a simple step for the common good that all other democracies have enacted.

Predictably, a solution to this problem has been advanced: to follow a guardian who will rescue us from the trap, from pluralism run amuck—the man on a white horse as the alterna-tive to the chaos and gridlock of democracy. In the tradition beginning with Plato, and running through to the long list of twentieth-century totalitarians, we are being told again that "leadership" will get us our fifty-cent gas tax.

Those who advance this line of reasoning are, like Plato, partly right in their reading of the problem and partly right in their solution, but both are based on the simplicity this side of

complexity, and thus must be rejected. In seeking to understand the complexity of this matter, one discovers that the same
charges now being brought against American democracy could
have been, and have been, levelled many other times in our
history. It turns out that a democracy is only beautiful when
viewed from a distance and over a very long period of time.
When examined up close and at any given moment, it is a
messy and dissatisfying thing, particularly when no immediate
crisis like a war is pulling everyone together in temporary consensus. At almost all other times, watching democracy in action
is like watching sausage being made, an unpretty process indeed.

A recent study by Yale political scientist David Mayhew,
Divided We Govern, shows that democratic gridlock is mainly
in the eyes of the beholder. Reviewing recent experience in
Washington, he demonstrates that legislative gridlock is more
myth than fact, even when the majority of the Congress are
from a different party than the president. What is typically seen
as gridlock is actually the process of consensus in the forging.
However, this study does not belie the fact of gridlock. It does
occur, and when it does the source has been leaders who are
ideologically unwilling to compromise. A major political phenomenon of the 1980s was the rise to power of individuals who
sought all or nothing. That was not the style of the four great
Presidents whose images are carved on Mount Rushmore.

Ironically, just as the peoples of eastern Europe are struggling to establish democracy, we Americans are discovering
that our own sausage factory is strewn with guts and gore. Just
as democracy has triumphed, dissatisfaction with the system is
growing among the very people who had been fighting to
spread it around the globe. Here the critics are partly right in
their diagnosis that the problem is, to a great degree, leadership. As Flora Lewis writes, "History does not just happen
and compel submission, it is made by men and women who

make decisions. Leaders are supposed to formulate and explain the decisions they consider best. Where are they? . . . Democracy is a process for correcting mistakes and making adjustments. It still needs ideas and public-spirited action."

The problem is, in part, the absence of leadership—but not the kind of leadership offered by Plato's guardians or this century's many men on white horses. Democratic leadership is not about power or authority; it is, as Lewis suggests, about identifying and communicating ideas. What are needed, in Madison's words, are leaders who "refine . . . the public views" and "discern the true interests" of the country. These leaders govern not by looking at the polls and then appealing to our basest instincts. Great leaders do indeed listen to their constituencies, but they are not slaves to public opinion. Instead, they "discern the true interests" of the nation by refining "the public views." Thus, the democratic leader's task is to invent policies that transcend the pettiness, contradictions, and self-interest revealed in public opinion. Such leaders are willing to ask the citizenry to sacrifice—in effect, to show the people why they have to pay the fifty-cent gas tax. Without doubt, this brand of leadership has been, at least temporarily, absent in America.

Was the democratic system, and is it still, capable of producing public-spirited leaders with transcendent ideas? Does history support the contention that pluralistic democracy tends in the direction of static compromise, or has the system actually fostered growth in the direction of the good society? To claim the latter, we must provide evidence that the laws and policies of government are, over time, expanding the central area of our quadrant by striking a creative balance between the four fundamental values of society—without creating a compromise that satisfies no one. Ultimately, there can be no objective proof of that proposition. To my mind, the mixed record of the American system offers enough examples of leaders with programs that simultaneously serve the ends of liberty, equality, efficiency, and community to pronounce the Madisonian experiment a success.

A measure of such balanced programs is that, once adopted, they cease to be controversial (for instance, they become as popular or unpopular with Libertarians as they are with Egalitarians). In the United States, the least controversial government programs have included universal public education (in concept, if not in execution); the formation of the land grant colleges; federal home loan policies prior to deregulation (which gave the working classes a stake in the system by making them property owners); and the G. I. Bill (which, in proper Millian fashion, married responsibilities to rights). Similarly, Depression-era public works programs were less controversial than contemporary welfare programs because they gave people the right to earn a living, as opposed to the right to a livelihood without a concomitant responsibility to work.

Well-designed programs directed toward ending discrimination in employment can increase efficiency while enhancing liberty, equality, and community. Other programs that expand the domains of all four values simultaneously include what Peter Drucker calls "pension fund socialism" (indirect employee stock ownership through institutional intermediaries), and what Louis Kelso and Mortimer Adler call "universal capitalism" (direct employee ownership in stock of the companies where they work).

Such policies are remarkable for the moral imagination displayed by their authors who, in each case, overcame ideology in quest of the good society. I suggest that the ability to find solutions to problems that simultaneously expand the realms of liberty, equality, efficiency, and community should be an essential component of any true definition of democratic leadership. That such leadership is not only possible, but that we have actually experienced it from time to time, is attested to by the following excerpt from a remarkable political address given by Theodore Roosevelt in a Kansas cornfield in 1910.

The fundamental thing to do for every man is to give him a chance to reach a place in which he will make the greatest possible contribution to the public welfare. Understand what I say here. Give him a chance, not push him up if he will not be pushed. Help any man who stumbles; if he lies down, it is a poor job to try to carry him; but if he is a worthy man, try your best to see that he gets a chance to show the worth that is in him. No man can be a good citizen unless he has a wage more than sufficient to cover the bare cost of living, and hours of labor short enough so that after his day's work is done he will have time and energy to share in the management of the community, to help in carrying the general load. We keep countless men from being good citizens by the conditions of life with which we surround them. We need comprehensive workmen's compensation acts, both state and national laws to regulate child labor and work for women, and, especially, we need in our common schools not merely education in book learning, but also practical training for daily life and work. We need to enforce better sanitary conditions for our workers and to extend the use of safety appliances for our workers in industry and commerce. . . . Also, friends, in the interest of the workingman himself we need to set our faces like flint against mob violence just as against corporate greed; against violence and injustice and lawlessness by wage workers just as much as against lawless cunning and greed and selfish arrogance of employers. If I could ask but one thing of my fellow countrymen, my request would be that, whenever they go in for reform, they remember the two sides, and that they always exact justice from one side as much as from the other. . . . If the reactionary man, who thinks of nothing but the right of property, could have his way, he would bring about a revolution; and one of my chief fears in connection with progress comes because I do not want to see our people, for lack of proper leadership, compelled to follow men whose intentions are excellent, but whose eyes are a little too wild to make it really safe to trust them. . . .

National efficiency has many factors. It is a necessary result of the principle of conservation widely applied. In the end it will determine our failure or success as a nation. National efficiency has to do, not only with natural resources and with men, but it is equally concerned with institutions. . . .

I do not ask for overcentralization; but I do ask that we work in a spirit of broad and far-reaching nationalism when we work for what concerns our people as a whole. We are all Americans.

In this speech Roosevelt displayed vision, integrity, and courage—essential traits of leadership in the democratic pursuit of balance between the four values he cites as equally important. Unfortunately, in recent years, democratic leadership has come to sound like an oxymoron to the ears of many Americans. If that is the case, then the observed immobilization of government and the growing collective cynicism in society are symptoms not of the failure of democracy but of the absence of leaders with sufficient moral imagination to overcome the countervailing ideological forces that are locked in stasis.

In the past, the great leaders of this democracy, like TR, understood that the pursuit of the good society requires addressing the conflicting demands of all individuals and groups. When a government does this well, the vast majority of its citizens view it as fair, just, and legitimate. Less good societies favor one ideology, one group, or one class and consequently are viewed as unjust, unfair, and illegitimate by those whose views and positions are unheard, unrespected, or ignored. Just societies are dynamic, complex, and multidimensional as they seek to respond to the many and changing needs of all their constituencies; the process of governance in unjust societies is static, simple, and one-dimensional. Such societies are brittle and ultimately break under the torque and tension of historical forces; just societies change, grow, and survive.

While everything may appear to run smoothly in a totalitarian state, the course of events in a democracy is continually bumpy. The perpetual lot of democracy is flux and spirited disagreement among those with competing values. The framers of America's democracy knew they were constructing no utopia. They saw that conflict, tension, and turmoil were the order of their day, and foresaw that they would be the order of the future as well. Indeed, they didn't see conflict as evil. (Jefferson relished it and saw it as the source of progress and continual change.)

What worried Madison and the other founders was that one party would emerge from the struggle as a permanent winner and other parties would be eternal losers. That loss, they feared, would not only destroy the moral basis of the union but could lead to tyranny. Such a possibility exists today, but in a way Madison never considered. For example, unlike the special-interest groups he described as continually realigning and recoalescing, racial minorities do not reconstitute themselves according to pluralistic theory; only moral leadership can prevent such groups from suffering possible tyranny at the hands of the permanent racial majority. Similarly, the current threat to a woman's right to terminate a pregnancy is a form of majority tyranny that Madison's theory did not anticipate. The founders did see, though, that they could not anticipate every issue likely to arise, so they built a change mechanism into the democracy they were inventing. In this pluralistic system, the founders thought the task of democratic leadership is to manage or balance the constant and never-abating demands of those with different dreams or values, not to define a single truth. Following Montesquieu, they did not believe that truth—in this instance, the concept of the good society—is eternal, static, or written. (Montesquieu wrote that law must be made with reference to the "humor and disposition of the people in whose favor it is established," and that this is unlikely to be the same in any two places or at any two times because laws "should be adapted in such a manner to the people for whom they are framed.")

What is the good society, then? The answer appears to be that it is a dynamic concept; the good society is what emerges over the long term from the continuous free interplay of competing ideas in a well-functioning democracy. As Lewis Lapham puts it, "The premise of American democracy assumes a raucous assembly of citizens unafraid to speak their minds."

≣ Future Agenda?

If the good society flows from the continuous and simultaneous pursuit of different values, and if the best process for managing that interplay is pluralistic democracy, then the continued pursuit of the good society requires full and true democracy. In point of fact, the political history of the West over the last two centuries has been characterized by the gradual expansion of the franchise, with subsequent addressing of the legitimate objectives of those who had lacked voice, power, and respect in the former systems. (TR was prescient on this score: had this process not occurred, Marx's prediction of the inevitable overthrow of the capitalist democracies probably would have come true). Today, however, only some 60 out of the approximately 180 independent nations of the world can be said to meet the requirements of a true democracy. These requirements are described by Robert A. Dahl in his recent book *Democracy and Its Critics,* in which he argues that high on the world's political agenda during the next century will be the transformation of the remaining two-thirds of all nations into democracies capable of pursuing the good society. He fears that process will be slow and painful.

Dahl also argues that the task of democratization in the West remains incomplete. One might cite as a symptom of this problem the fact that the rate of participation in democratic processes is on the decline in almost all the advanced Western nations. Each year, fewer and fewer citizens vote, and still fewer participate directly in grass roots political activity. Consider that TR's cornfield audience in 1910 consisted of farmers, workers, and small business proprietors, many of whom then gathered after the address to debate among themselves the issues Roosevelt had raised. That happens seldom today. Part of the problem is television, which has turned politics into a spectator sport for couch potatoes, one in which nothing is required of the viewer but to stay awake; with the analysis of issues reduced to thirty-second sound bites, even that is not much of a challenge. The growth of mindless television damages democracy in other ways, as well. Democracy requires an informed and demanding citizenry, not the kind of nonvoter who, in an interview on MTV during the 1992 election, explained, "Voting isn't in my space."

In addition to being informed and exercising the right to vote, the electorate has the responsibility from time to time to vote out the incumbents. This periodic necessity constitutes the "little rebellion" that Jefferson called "a good thing and as necessary in the political world as storms in the physical." We should not confuse "Throwing the bums out," though, with throwing democracy out; in fact, it is an exercise in making democracy work. Oddly, in America we have confused these two quite different courses of action.

For current problems of American democracy, a part of the remedy lies within ourselves, a part with getting good leaders, a part with the media, a part with education, and a part with reforms of the system. On retiring in disgust from the U.S. Senate in 1992, Senator Timothy Wirth wrote, "The public interest requires an interested public, candidates who treat voters as responsible adults and a press, as the fourth branch of government, that gives the substance of campaigns the same scrutiny as the contestants' private lives and finances. That should not be too much to ask of the world's oldest democracy."

Wirth's demands are reasonable, indeed, but a major stumbling block stands in their way. That discouraging obstacle is the fact that money has become, in the words of a late California politician, "the mother's milk of politics." With

PACs and special-interest groups funding incumbents' television spots, average voters feel they have lost their political voice, power, and respect. To the citizenry, politics today seems more about lawyers, public relations firms, and high-priced lobbyists than individual voters. The money needed to buy television has also made the two major political parties reliant on the same special-interest contributors, a tie that blurs distinctions between them and disintegrates the ties of loyalty that once bound them to the people. As a result, the parties have lost their purpose and punch. Those who see parties as dirty and divisive remnants of Tammany Hall and Chicago ward bossism call the development progress. In fact, it is a step backward because representative democracy cannot function without parties, as Jefferson was forced to admit late in his life after having been the nation's most outspoken critic of party politics. In sum, much that is wrong with democracy could be cured by the removal of a great deal of mischief-making money. Since so much of this money originates in the business sector, this appears to be an area where corporate leadership would be particularly appropriate and effective. The professional and occupational special groups who are also large campaign donors and could be shamed into following the corporate lead.

If these are the problems, then the marked dissatisfaction with the system noted on the first page of this book is the result not of too much democracy, but too little. That shortfall would explain why so many citizens still complain of injustices even though they possess the franchise and all its associated rights and freedoms. The desire for more democracy was made manifest during the 1992 presidential campaign, when there was overwhelming popular consensus that the highpoint of that rather low campaign was a debate in which the candidates were questioned by common citizens. In the 1980s, a number of critics took this observation and used it as the basis of a wrong-headed attack on American democracy. Alvin Toffler posited—

and Ross Perot advanced the argument—that it is *representative* democracy, in particular, which is unresponsive to the electorate and which leads to the observed paralysis of government. The antidote they proposed was direct electronic plebiscites, which would reduce voter apathy, eliminate lobbyists and party middlemen, and produce decisions that would flow directly from the will of the people in the nationwide equivalent of a New England town meeting.

There is long-standing fascination with the promise of plebiscitory democracy (apparently, getting rid of politicians is almost as attractive as the prospect of doing away with lawyers). Sociologist Max Weber, who had been the author of the failed Weimar Constitution, argued that he would much have preferred a plebiscitory system under a strong leader to the weak and corrupt parliamentary system that he had designed. Of course, Weber did not live to see the strong man who arose out of the ashes of Weimar.

Does direct democracy expand freedom, or does it just give the appearance of doing so because it is so efficient? Who, for example, will phrase the questions on which we must vote? Who will choose when to hold a plebiscite? Such unanswerable questions suggest the possibility that electronic plebiscites may, indeed, be more effectively manipulated than is the messy and slow system of representive democracy.

The new technology would doubtless abet and exacerbate the current problem of single-issue politics. There would be ready manipulation by the committed and little protection for minority opinion. As much as one may dislike political parties, they do force trade-offs, compromise, accommodation, cooperation, and the safeguarding of minority rights—which is, of course, the essence of justice in a pluralistic democracy. Parties, for all their manifest faults, force consensus. Plebiscites, in contrast, create polarization.

Electronic plebiscites would also spread the dreaded California Syndrome to the rest of the nation. In California, voters are forced to make dozens—sometimes as many as four or five dozen—separate and "informed" decisions about confusingly worded city, county, and state propositions. California's voters are complaining that they do not want this mere appearance of democracy. Instead, they call for an end to being manipulated by the special interests who use the inability of the voters to make sense out of a welter of confusion to their own selfish ends. California's voters are starting to demand that their representatives do the job for which they were elected: the task of deliberation, debate, consensus building, and choice.

If we wish to have a preview of TV democracy we need only tune in on Sunday morning to the contentious rabble-rousing of the "McLaughlin Group." Any sensible citizen would prefer the slow, inefficient, elitist, gridlocked club called the U.S. Senate. Again, the dissatisfaction with gridlock is, in most instances, misplaced frustration with the slow process of pluralistic, representative democracy. As Weimar Germany discovered after it was too late, it is foolish in the extreme to attempt to make democracy more "efficient." The dissatisfaction can only be removed by political leaders who establish the civic virtues— the shared democratic values—that Havel identifies.

Another explanation for the observed dissatisfaction, according to Dahl, is the fact that government is not the only power center in modern dynamic pluralistic societies; the policies of private organizations also affect perceptions of the goodness of society. He argues that the next stage of democratization in the West will be the devolution of authority in workplaces.

> I have no doubt that many people will immediately reject the idea of extending the democratic process to business firms as foolish and unrealistic. It may therefore be helpful to recall that not long ago most people took it as a matter of self-evident good sense that the idea of applying the democratic process to the government of the nation-state was foolish and unrealistic.

In particular, this foolish and unrealistic notion was derided by those who believed that wisdom rests with an elite group of guardians. Dahl says that not only has this belief been belied for society as a whole, it is also not true inside work organizations. He argues that participative organizations would be more effective (and be viewed as more legitimate) than those managed by a small class of expert guardians. Recent organizational research that demonstrates the peculiar effectiveness and productivity of highly decentralized, participative companies, particularly those with high levels of employee ownership, seems to support Dahl's point.

Let us be clear about this: The day when people in work organizations will have the vote is far off—after all, it took twenty-five hundred years for everyone to become politically enfranchised. As the Chairman of the Herman Miller corporation, Max De Pree, explains about his own highly participative company, "Everyone has the right and the duty to influence decision making and to understand the results. Participative management guarantees that decisions will not be arbitrary, secret, or closed to questioning. Participative management is not democratic. Having a say differs from having a vote." At any rate, voting is not necessary in most organizations and is almost always undesirable; voting makes sense within a sovereign nation but is far less useful in other contexts. As the American statesman Harlan Cleveland writes about the United Nations, "Voting is a good way to take a snapshot of disagreement; but voting is not very useful in bonding sovereign peoples to do something together." Cleveland argues that, outside of sovereign nations, we should be talking not about voting but the fostering of "democratic values," the foremost of which is a commitment to human rights.

To this end, Max De Pree has taken the same first step toward democracy inside his organization that the Enlightenment philosophers took long prior to the introduction of political democracy: He has acknowledged that his employees have rights. "Each of us, no matter what our rank in the hierarchy may be, has the same rights: to be needed, to be involved, to have a covenantal relationship, to understand the corporation, to be accountable, to appeal." Echoing Vaclav Havel, what workplaces need is a civic culture characterized by the values of democratic pluralism: decency, reason, responsibility, tolerance, and human rights.

If Dahl is correct, and if the ideas of De Pree and others who think like him spread, managers in the future can look forward to the tensions between the four dominant values of society being played out through pluralistic processes *within* their organizations, and to confronting the same daunting challenges of democratic leadership with which officials in the public sector currently struggle. The future of the corporation may then become as full of continuing stress, conflict, disagreement, competing interests, divergent goals, contradictions, self-doubt, and self-criticism as the modern democratic state! Doubtless most managers will resist such a prospect. Paradoxically, though, if Dahl's equation of the nation to the corporation holds, that future might in fact be a bright one for the corporation. One lesson we have learned in the last few tumultuous years is that nondemocratic nations under the command and control of guardians have been totally incapable of coping with the complexities of change, while democracies have not only adapted but thrived. In the long term, the democratic pursuit of the good society seems to make sound practical sense.

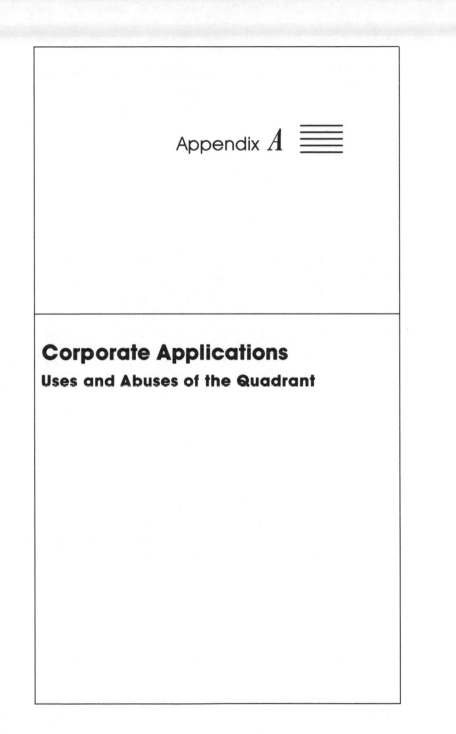

Appendix A

Corporate Applications
Uses and Abuses of the Quadrant

The values quadrant serves a function similar to that of a compass card on a map: It is an instrument that aids in the determination of direction. Once we understand the philosophies represented by each polar point, one may use the quadrant, somewhat in the manner of a compass in the sport of orienteering, to discover where one is in relation to the beliefs and values of others, and to see where one stands in a larger scheme. In the words of the German sociologist Karl Mannheim, the quadrant addresses the confusion caused by the "multiplicity of points of view" that prevent us from seeing "the whole." In 1936, Mannheim speculated that the world crisis then brewing stemmed, in large part, from the inability of people to see beyond "their narrow and particularized positions"—they were blind to "any larger context." The heterogeneous peoples of Europe could not see the validity of the different perspectives, positions, needs, values, and experiences of others. Mannheim worried that the dictators of the era would seize upon this ethnocentric blindness and use it as a pretext for great mischief. Mannheim wrote that the imminent requirement was for a greater "comprehension of the whole," by which "the individual learns to orient himself beyond the narrow horizon of his home town and learns to understand himself as part of a national and, later, a world situation." Such understanding came too late to avoid the horrors of World War II.

Today, conflicts rooted in a diversity of values continue to indicate the need for the kind of social orienteering Mannheim advocated. During the last two decades the values quadrant has been used profitably for various forms of social and political orienteering, by individuals (corporate executives, entrepreneurs, professionals, and MBA students) and by organizations (corporations, nonprofits, and universities). The range I will describe of these applications—personal and professional, developmental and practical—is meant to be illustrative, not inclusive. The imaginative manager doubtless will find other useful applications for the tool.

Nonetheless, a tool is useful only for certain purposes; as useful as a hammer is, it cannot be used to saw wood or drive screws. Similarly, the use of the quadrant has many limitations. It helps us to understand the nature of the good society, but it tells us little about the nature of the good person. It is nearly useless as a psychological instrument, for it fails to account for such significant emotional considerations as self-esteem and the desire for power. Equally, it is not helpful in the analysis of religious concerns (or prejudices).

It is worth keeping in mind that the values quadrant is merely a representation of one important aspect of social reality, a kind of visual metaphor of the political economy. The north and south points on the compass card are not literally polar opposites anymore than a picture of a pipe is a pipe or my love is a rose. And there is no true north to be found in the social affairs of humankind. Furthermore, the compass card is, by necessity of the printed page, a flat representation of a concept that should be visualized as three-dimensional; until this book finds its way onto a CD in the next generation of telecomputers, readers may find it useful to visualize the poles as force fields.

Furthermore, a real compass has 360 degrees, and we have identified only four points on our values quadrant. I am confident that a more imaginative and energetic soul than I could generate defensible descriptive titles for the remaining 356 currently nameless positions around the circle. As important as it is to acknowledge their existence, however, I am not certain the exercise of naming them all would be particularly useful. Our compass simply is not a precise instrument. That is why no warrant is offered as to its scientific validity. (Those concerned with instrument validation may find some benefit in perusing my article "What's Ahead for the Business/Government Relationship" in the March-April 1979 issue of the *Harvard Business Review,* which gives a bit of empirical evidence that leaders from various sectors of society tend to cluster themselves predictably along our four ideological dimensions.)

Whatever validity the compass possesses derives from its logical integrity and its perceived usefulness. Numerous applications of the tool over the last two decades reveal an interesting phenomenon: Individuals who are the most absolute in their ideological orientations are the most likely to reject the overall validity of the quadrant's logic. Why this is so is a bit puzzling. Must those who are rigid in their thinking deny the legitimacy of others' values in order to cope with cognitive dissonance? For example, at one Aspen seminar, an economist trained at the University of Chicago initially refused to take part in discussions of the quadrant unless his fellow participants agreed to label LIBERTY as true north and to write the names of the three other values in lower case! At another seminar, a self-described radical feminist, who had volunteered that her beliefs put her in the extreme corner of the southwest quadrant, rejected the logic of the compass because the authorities cited for all four positions were predominantly dead white males. The other seminarians ultimately persuaded her to take part in the discussion, arguing that the purpose of the exercise was a historical analysis of the origins of democratic capitalism, a process that had wrongly excluded the majority of the world's population. Once persuaded that their exercise was based on what was, and not on what should be, she pitched in and usefully identified where contemporary writers, especially women and people of color, might be placed on the compass. Neither of these instances belie the validity of the compass; both instances prove its usefulness as an educational tool in clarifying real and important differences in values.

≡ Personal Uses

In numerous applications, the values compass has proved useful to individuals in formulating relatively precise answers to the following kinds of questions:

Where am I? When first used by my MBA students in the 1970s, the vast majority would identify their beliefs as being in the NE quadrant; as environmental concerns surfaced in the early 1990s, a (bare) majority began to identify themselves as being in the NW quadrant. (Of course, the current "politically correct" stance on campus is in the SW quadrant, but few business students claim that particular territory.) Wherever one chooses to stand, the ability to clearly identify one's own political/economic values in this way is an important aspect of political and social self-awareness.

Where are my opponents? In formulating a negotiation strategy it is useful to know where the opposition is coming from. One's approach might differ greatly if the disagreement is profound and based on ideological ends, as opposed to being more bridgeable and based only on differing means to a mutually sought end. Tolerance may also be a useful by-product of understanding the motivations of others.

Where is this or that country? Maoist China was manifestly at the south pole of the quadrant. Until recently, post–World War II Japan has been close to the efficiency pole on the horizontal axis, community being more important to the Japanese than either liberty or equality. Sweden, under the Social Democrats, was somewhere near the center, perhaps in the SW quadrant, having moved a bit into the lower corner of the NE quadrant as a result of the recent election of a nonsocialist government. Arguably, the United States has always been in the NE quadrant, although there has been considerable migration within that territory over our history, as illustrated.

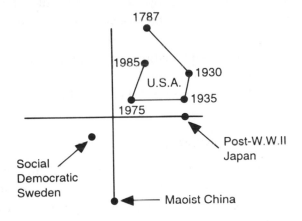

At the time the Constitution was framed, the policies of the United States were decidedly Libertarian. By the end of the Industrial Revolution, the nation had acquired a marked Corporatist tinge. New Deal legislation moved the country a bit southward toward Egalitarianism. In the 1970s, with the formation of the Environmental Protection Agency, there was a clear migration in the direction of the Communitarian pole. Finally, the election of Ronald Reagan pushed the country back toward its Libertarian beginnings. All these shifts, though, have been constrained by the attraction of the value of liberty. In this respect, our University of Chicago economist was correct: in the United States, liberty represents the kind of powerful force that the North Pole exerts on a true compass. By no means is this a universal phenomenon, however. As we have seen, for most of the world prior to the eighteenth century, community was far and away the polar value of greatest strength.

Where do I have to go to get what I want? The quadrant's eastern hemisphere contains economic concerns, and its western hemisphere contains social goods. (Liberty and equality have both economic and social dimensions.) As we have noted, trade-offs along the horizontal and vertical axes are more pronounced than trade-offs between adjoining values. For example, there is more compatibility among liberty and efficiency than between liberty and equality, and more compatibility between community and equality than between community and efficiency. We are, thus, more likely to find people who are Libertarian/Corporatists than Libertarian/Egalitarians.

≡ Corporate Applications

Over the last two decades, executives, management consultants and educators have used the quadrant for a variety of organizational purposes. One was a manufacturing firm that had been planning to build a state-of-the-art factory until its executives became concerned that the racial, cultural, and educational diversity of the new work force might make the levels of productivity that engineers had projected difficult to achieve. The executives feared that, if the various and differing needs of the work force were not addressed, an unproductive state of conflict would exist inside the plant instead of a productive sense of community. To address this problem, a planning team was formed consisting of representatives of the architects, engineers, operations managers, union officials, and workers who would be involved both in building and in operating the plant. Before they turned to practical questions of plant layout, staffing levels, process technology and job design, they devoted a day to a discussion of the four poles of a just society.

In light of this shared experience and vocabulary, the team found that their subsequent discussions of such issues as work rules were shaped by a heightened sensitivity to questions of value differences. They kept raising the following kinds of concerns: "Have we accounted for all the technological, economic, political, and human variables in our plans?" "Have we accommodated the concerns of all the participants in the process?" In the end, the parties involved felt they had engaged in a community-building exercise that harmonized the potentially conflicting ends sought by various groups into shared values.

When dealing with such human resource questions, several companies have attempted to translate the social and political values of the quadrant into organization and management values. Four extreme management philosophies have been found to map onto the political ideologies we have discussed. *Meritocracy* is the belief that corporations must be structured to reflect the real differences between individual ability, talent, and willingness to work. Meritocratic organizations have extremely high pay differentials between jobs at the top of the hierarchy and at the bottom, and mobility up the corporate ladder is rapid for the most successful performers. *Egalitarianism* is the belief that employees should be protected against nearly every form of risk by numerous entitlements and limits on managerial discretion. In such organizations, workers have guaranteed job security and are paid as equally as possible. *Behaviorism* is the belief that jobs should be narrow in scope and engineered for maximum efficiency. Such organizations monitor performance closely and have an elaborate incentive system providing frequent rewards for the most efficient workers. *Humanism* is the belief that organizational policies and practices should enhance the personal growth of all employees. In such organizations workers have extensive ownership, participation in decisionmaking, and career-long learning. These four schools of managerial thought correspond to the political values quadrant:

MERITOCRACY
(Merit and Freedom)

HUMANISM   *vs.*   BEHAVIORISM
(Quality of Worklife)   *(Efficiency and Order)*

EGALITARIANISM
(Security and Equality)

Those who translate the quadrant concept in this fashion do so in the belief that the good organization simultaneously pursues as much merit, as much efficiency, as much security, and as high a quality of work life as it can obtain. In effect, organizational effectiveness equates with the balance found in the good society. While many companies report success using the quadrant in this manner, I confess I have had mixed results when I have attempted to do so. To my mind, the parallels between the external and internal environments of organizations aren't exact enough to make such a translation fully convincing.

A large entertainment conglomerate used the political values quadrant in a quite different fashion—as a tool for defining their social mission and public responsibilities. Before sitting down to write a nuts-and-bolts statement of corporate social policy, the firm's top management engaged in a two-and-a-half day mini–Aspen Executive Seminar, discussing many of the readings reviewed in these pages. At the end of it they asked themselves two questions: "What is the good society?" and "What is the role of a large, publicly held corporation in achieving the elements of that society?" A few weeks later they reconvened and addressed their practical agenda. In light of their previous discussions they asked, "What is the particular role of our company in securing the good society?" and "What particular responsibilities and competencies do we possess when it comes to helping others to achieve social justice?"

They discovered that the most practical way they could approach the issues of pluralism raised in their previous, philosophical discussions was to identify, and seek to address, the values and needs of their numerous stakeholders.

An industrial conglomerate that had experienced a series of minor, but potentially costly, ethical problems found in the quadrant a useful way to bring a sharp focus to workshops they had set up to deal with moral issues. Discussions of the quadrant helped them create a framework for understanding and clarifying the differences between right and wrong. They identified the area in the center of the quadrant as "virtue," and proceeded to identify steps the organization could take to encourage virtuous behavior on the part of all employees.

Other organizations have used discussions of the quadrant as a way of expanding their existing frames of reference in strategic planning exercises, and as preludes to such activities as the analysis of changing market demographics, and to policy debates on such trade-offs as shareowner rights versus long-term investment or the formation of PACs versus employee rights. (One can intuit how the quadrant might be used for such purposes; I do not have reliable information about how successful these exercises were in practice.)

I am most familiar with the use of the quadrant in the Wider Dimension program of the Institute for Information Studies. Several times a year for the last several years, this joint program of the Aspen Institute and the Northern Telecom corporation has engaged Northern's corporate customers in discussions about the policy implications of emerging telecommunications technologies. In one exercise, participants study and evaluate four untitled proposals that represent the divergent ideological positions of four fictitious politicians. These proposals are written in the form of congressional testimony, with each politician advocating a different national policy on telecommunications and information technology. (For examples, see Appendix B). Institute participants are asked to create a short, descriptive title for each proposal. (One validation of the exercise is the fact that the majority of participants nominate, unprompted, such titles as Free Market and Laissez Faire for the Libertarian proposal.) They are then asked to offer a personal assessment of the desirability of each proposal on a scale of zero (totally unacceptable from their point of view) to one hundred (their ideal).

A staff member then leads the group in a discussion of the four proposals, asking the following kinds of questions with regard to each in turn:

"Did anyone give this proposal a high rating? If so, why? What would be the positive consequences of this proposal?"

"Did anyone give this proposal a low rating? If so, why? What would be the negative consequences of this proposal?"

"In this proposal, who benefits and who loses?"

"What was the goal of the author of this proposal?"

"What title did you give it? Why?"

"Who, or what groups, in our society are proponents of this point of view?"

The discussion leader draws the values quadrant on a blackboard pole-by-pole as the discussion proceeds, leaving ample time and room for the participants not only to express their personal values but to identify the values of the advocates of each proposal. The leader then turns to a general discussion of the now completed quadrant, raising such questions as

"Which value, or values, should society pursue?"

"Where is justice on the quadrant?"

"Why is the nation having trouble achieving consensus on these policy issues?"

"What does our discussion suggest about the ways our own supposedly technical concerns are fraught with ideology and values?"

The Institute for Information Studies has had success using the quadrant not only with businesspeople and technicians but also with educators and health care professionals. For example, with educators, after a brief discussion of the quadrant, they ask the following kinds of questions:

"How can liberty in education be enhanced by technology?"

"How can liberty in education be undermined by that same technology?"

All this said and done, in the end it doesn't really matter how corporations use the quadrant, or even if they use it at all. What matters is that executives read, think, and talk with others about the great ideas of political economy. It is particularly useful for us to discuss these ideas with people from diverse backgrounds, because our goal is to free ourselves from our narrow and particularized positions and to expand our comprehension of the whole. However we go about doing that, the beneficiaries will be ourselves, our organizations, and the larger community of which we are all a part.

Appendix B

Four Proposals

**An Exercise in Applying the Ideas
in This Book to a Contemporary Debate**

☰ Telecommunications/Information Technology Policy: The Tension among Fundamental Values

Instructions

Our purpose is to consider how complex and far reaching technological issues are resolved by public policy debate and decisions calculated to achieve the most productive and beneficial impacts on all sectors of society.

The scenarios that follow represent the expressed views of four politicians who are articulate advocates of differing positions regarding a possible telecommunications/information technology policy.

After reading, give each statement a short descriptive title. (One could be called the "Liberal Proposal" and another the "Conservative Proposal," but since we have now used those

Source: The Institute for Information Studies

two labels as examples, you must come up with other—even more descriptive—one or two word titles!).

Based on your own judgment, please offer a personal assessment of the desirability of each proposal on a scale of ZERO (a totally unacceptable policy from your point of view) to ONE HUNDRED (the ideal policy in your eyes). The combined score of all four proposals need not add up to one hundred.

Do not agonize over the details of the proposals. Just spend a couple of minutes with each and go with your instincts.

≣ Proposal A

The ——— *Position*

It is clear from the testimony we have heard that *no policy* is the best plan. In the telecommunications/computers arena, governmental power represents too great a threat to freedom to warrant tinkering with the naturally efficient workings of the market. By itself, competition provides all the regulation and incentives for innovation that are required. Consequently, we should move as quickly as possible to deregulate the telecommunications industries. What business is it of government who owns what television or radio station? As for programming and forms of delivery, the rule should be: the consumer is king. It is up to the public to decide what they watch in the privacy of their own homes: whether it is brought by cable, broadcast, satellite or on phone lines, the public must be free to choose both the method of delivery and the content of the programs. For example, the U.S. government should have left AT&T to its own devices—allowing the introduction of new technology to attack its monopoly (if, indeed, that is what the market mechanism had dictated).

In the computer-related fields, the genius of entrepreneurs and inventors will meet the challenge of competition *if* they are freed from excessive regulation and taxation. While the full list of government infringements on the workings of the market would fill a book, we must begin to remove these by abolishing all tariffs, quotas and controls on the sale and transfer of technology and capital to enterprises and to governments. Domestically, we should unleash the powers of entrepreneurs by eliminating capital gains taxes, and by reducing taxes on income to the level prescribed by logic of supply side economics.

History shows that the only impediments to innovation, growth and the creation of wealth are the well-meaning and do-good interference of government into the wealth-creating activities of capitalists. Equally important, the emerging telecommunication/computer devices are technologies of political freedom: they promise to free peoples everywhere from network journalists. In the future, these technologies will allow for direct national plebiscites, thus freeing the public from the stranglehold of political parties and professional politicians. Thus, the proper role of government is to deregulate, encourage competition and limit the sphere of governmental authority to enforcing contracts between consenting adults.

≣ Proposal B

The ——— Position

It is clear from the testimony we have heard that fairness requires us to establish an industrial policy for telecommunications along the lines of the "indicative planning" model found in the social democracies of Western Europe. While the market plays a role in such systems, the government does those things that the market fails to do. Left to its own devices, the market creates unjust disparities between the winners and losers in society and creates imbalances between classes, races and geographical regions. The market also fails to account for the long term.

It was for these reasons that our predecessors established regulatory agencies to deal with the telecom industry. For example, in the United States, AT&T was allowed its monopoly in a fair exchange with society for high levels of service, access to the poor and to rural regions, low prices and research in the national interest. This was a good bargain, and should not have been altered. Accordingly, we must regulate the access to and ownership of television and radio stations. In order to increase the amount of public service programming and to ensure fairness, we must extend regulatory jurisdiction to cable and to other narrowcast technologies. In sum, we must resist the growing pressures to deregulate. The telecommunication and computer industries are already the least-regulated in the world; in fact, we should be going the other way, creating common technical standards, providing access to high-tech goods and services for the culturally and economically disadvantaged and, in general, assuring that these resources will serve the common good rather than the interests of the rich and powerful.

In order to allow corporations to compete successfully—and, thus, create jobs—we must maintain tariff and other barriers against unfair competition. Moreover, we must follow the example of Japan and Europe and invest in promising new technologies to give all corporations a jump-start in global competition. Governments must thus invest in the industrial infrastructure of telecommunications, much as the French have done with Minitel. And, like the German Max Planck Institutes, we should create government-funded, independent non-defense related high-tech research centers. Moreover, we must support science and math education in schools and colleges. In particular, we should offer scholarships to encourage the culturally and economically disadvantaged to enter these fields. Not only must the government assure that all have equal opportunity to learn the new high tech skills, it must insure that all have equal access to the new technologies which, because of their importance, are a public and not simply a private concern. Thus, we must balance the economic power of large corporations with the political power of government.

≣ Proposal C

The ——— Position

It is clear from the testimony that we have heard that we should establish something like the Japanese Ministry of International Trade and Industry. The proper role of government is to serve the needs of business in the tough world of international competition in which it is Japan, Inc. and EEC, Inc. against the rest of us. The goal should be to make industry as efficient as possible vis-à-vis our competitors. To achieve that end, we must play the game by their rules. First we must end the fiction that anti-trust laws encourage efficient competition. In fact, large corporations must be allowed to combine in order to achieve the economies of scale necessary to meet foreign, government-supported, giant corporations. As a first step, corporations should be allowed to pool R&D, technology and markets.

To increase productivity and our standard of living, we must get government on the side of business. That means that all well-meaning environmental, consumerist, labor and other regulations that hamper competitiveness should be reviewed by joint business-government panels. Indeed, all adversarial governmental agencies should be changed to operate in consultation with industry. Because economic growth is in the interest of all, investment tax credits must either be greatly increased or corporate income taxes removed entirely. It is also clear that something like a moon shot high-tech program is needed. While Minitel is one model, such a program should be accomplished through a consortium of private telecommunications and computer firms to avoid the inefficiencies of French-style state bureaucracies. The basic research for the program could be underwritten by government funds. Government should also pay for programs to retrain workers for high-tech and telecommunication industries. The program would be administered by the corporate sector. Most important, the costs of products must be reduced through improved engineering and management methods. Government should work with business and education to ensure a supply of high-tech engineers and others trained in such new productivity techniques as just-in-time, total quality management, and numerical controls.

A major problem all high-tech firms face is the unpredictability of the regulatory environment. By insuring that all federal agencies are staffed by people with business experience, some of the current unpredictability of government actions can be reduced. The real issues aren't whether the position of the big broadcast networks should be maintained, or whether other large organizations should be broken up, as was AT&T in the United States; rather, we must create policy which provides that all such decisions will be made rationally and carefully by business-oriented panels as opposed to being made by anti-business judges and bureaucrats.

≡ **Proposal D**

The —— *Position*

It is clear from the testimony that our policy needs to reflect the new global paradigm. The world is now one, and it is no longer "Us vs. Them." Thus, we must learn to think globally while we act locally. Thinking globally requires considering not only the environmental impact of our actions, but the effects of the new technologies on Third World employment, development and dependency. For example, in the emerging knowledge economy, the unskilled of the Third World may be left behind as a permanent underclass. International efforts must be mounted to address such problems, including issues like the call from the information-poor for a global information order.

Acting locally, we must establish decentralized, participatory offices of technology assessment around the country. While most environmental and social consequences of telecom/ computer technologies *appear* benign, they could present a threat to such values as privacy, community and local control. What is worrying is that public policy in this area will be made solely on economic and technological considerations, while human issues will be ignored. Farsight is needed with all technology. The intent is not to stifle the introduction of technology but to insure that it serves human ends. Thus, we should err towards policies based on the beliefs that small is better than big, decentralized better than centralized, local better than national, participation better than diktat, demassified better than standardized, and community-centered uses better than self-interested ones. For example, since it is unknown if working with computers is bad for one's health, if the by-products in the manufacture of semiconducters are dangerous, or if watching television predisposes youth toward violence, it is prudent to be safe in the short-term rather than sorry in the long-run. Is it not better to let the local community decide whether it wants to provide access to certain kinds of commercial or public-service television programming?

Since human development should take precedence over economic development, technology policy should seek to empower the culturally and economically disadvantaged within all regulatory bodies, broadcast licensees, and private companies under contract to the government (and to favor worker-owned licensees and contractors). In particular, policy must weigh against the dehumanizing aspects of the new "technologies of control." In workplaces, "smart machines" can be either enslaving *or* empowering; we must encourage the latter. Huxley showed how the new technologies can create a sense of powerlessness, wantonness and rootlessness—values we are exporting to the Third World via television programs. And Orwell showed the threats to privacy and democracy that can result from technology as apparently "innocent" as Minitel. In sum, one needn't be a Luddite to be on the guard against technological dehumanization.

Bibliography

Liberty

Basic Readings

"An Agreement of the People" [Debate between Cromwellians and the Levellers]." In *Puritanism and Liberty*, ed. A. S. P. Woodhouse, 1938.

The Constitution of the United States, 1787.

"Debate in the 1821 New York Constitutional Convention." In *Reports of the Proceedings and Debates of the Convention of 1821 Assembled for the Purpose of Amending the Constitution of the State of New York*, 1821.

Boucher, Jonathan. "On Civil Liberty, Passive Obedience and Resistance." In *A View of the Causes and Consequences of the American Revolution with an Historical Preface*, 1797.

Calhoun, John C. "The True Nature of Constitutional Government." In *Works*, vol. 1, 1855.

Kant, Immanuel. *The Science of Right*, 1785.

Locke, John. *The Second Treatise on Government*, chs. II, IV, XV, and XIX, 1689.

Mill, J. S. *On Liberty*, 1859.

Smith, Adam. *The Wealth of Nations*, 1776.

Sophocles. "Antigone."

Spencer, Herbert. *The Man Versus the State*, 1884.

Sumner, William Graham. "The Challenge of Facts." In *The Challenge of Facts and Other Essays*, ed. Albert Keller, 1914.

Contemporary Libertarianism

Friedman, Milton. *Capitalism and Freedom,* 1962.
Hayek, Friedrich A. von. *The Road to Serfdom,* 1944.
Rand, Ayn. *The Fountainhead,* 1943.
Schumpeter, Joseph. *Capitalism, Socialism and Democracy,* 1947.

Equality

Basic Readings

The Declaration of Independence, 1776.
"Preamble of the Mechanics' Union of Trade Associations, 1827." In
    A Documentary History of American Industrial Society, ed. John
    R. Commons et al., vol. V, 1910.
Aristotle. *Politics,* bk. I, chs. 8–13.
Franklin, Benjamin. "On the Legislative Branch." From *Representa-
    tion and Suffrage* in *The Complete Works,* ed. John Bigelow,
    vol. X, 1888.
George, Henry. *Progress and Poverty,* 1926.
King, Martin Luther, Jr. "Letter from a Birmingham City Jail," 1963.
Locke, John. *The Second Treatise of Government,* ch. V, 1689.
Mann, Horace. "The Importance of Universal, Free, Public Educa-
    tion," *Lectures and Annual Reports on Education,* ed. Mary
    Mann, vol. III, 1867.
Marx, Karl, and Friedrich Engels. *The Communist Manifesto,* 1847.
Melville, Herman. *Billy Budd,* 1924.
Mill, Harriet Taylor. "Enfranchisement of Women." In *Dissertations
    and Discussions,* ed. John Stuart Mill, vol. 2. 4 Vols., 1859–75.
Roosevelt, Franklin D. "The Commonwealth Club Address, 1932."
    In *Public Papers and Addresses,* vol. 1, 1938.
———. "1944 State of the Union Message."
Rousseau, Jean Jacques. *The Social Contract,* bk. I, selection 9, 1762.
Ryan, John A. *A Living Wage,* 1906.
Tawney, R. H. *Equality,* 1929.
"To Secure These Rights." *The Report of the President's [Truman]
    Committee on Civil Rights,* 1947.
Wallace, Henry. "An Economic Bill of Rights." *New York Times,*
    January 26, 1945.
Woolf, Virginia. *A Room of One's Own,* 1929.

Contemporary Egalitarianism (Social Democratic Variety)

Friedan, Betty. *The Feminine Mystique*, 1963.
Harrington, Michael. *The Other America*, 1962.
Okun, Arthur. *Equality and Efficiency: The Big Tradeoff*, 1975.
Rawls, John. *A Theory of Justice*, 1971.

Efficiency

Basic Readings

Confucius. *Analects*.
Hamilton, Alexander. "Report on Manufactures, December, 1791."
    In *Reports of the Secretary of the Treasury of the United States*,
    vol. I, 1837.
Hobbes, Thomas. *Leviathan*, chs. XIII, XIV, XV, and XVII, 1651.
Keynes, J. M. *The General Theory*, 1935–36.
Machiavelli, Niccolo. *The Prince*, 1513.
Plato. *The Republic*.
Simon, Herbert. *Administrative Behavior*, 1957.
Sloan, Alfred. *My Years With General Motors*, 1963.
Thucydides. "The Melian Conference," In *The Peloponnesian War*,
    ch. XVII.

Contemporary Corporatism

Galbraith, J. K. *The New Industrial State*, 1967.
Kobayashi, Yotaro. "A Message to American Managers." *Gaiko Fo-rum* (November 1989).
Reich, Robert. *The Work of Nations*, 1992.
Thurow, Lester. *Head to Head: The Coming Economic Battle Among Japan, Europe, and America*, 1992.

Community

Basic Readings

Aristotle. *Politics*, bk. I, chs. 1–7.
The Bible. Genesis I–IV.
Darwin, Charles. "The Development of a Moral Sense in Man." In
    The Descent of Man, chs. IV and XXI, 1871.

Jefferson, Thomas. Letter to Benjamin Austin, January 9, 1816. In *The Writings of Thomas Jefferson*, ed. H. A. Washington, vol. VI, 1861.

———. "The Merits of Agriculture." In *Notes on the State of Virginia*, 1787.

Owen, Robert. *A New View of Society*, 1813.

Rousseau, Jean Jacques. *The Social Contract*, bk. I, selections 1–8, 1762.

Takeo, Doi. "*Amae*: A Key Concept for Understanding Japanese Personality." In *Japanese Culture: Its Development and Characteristics*, ed. R. J. Smith and R. K. Beardsley, 1962.

Tocqueville, Alexis de. *Democracy in America*, bk. 1, ch. 15 and Conclusion, 1835; bk. 2, chs. 1, 2, 4, 5, and 6, 1840.

Veblen, Thorstein. *Theory of the Leisure Class*, 1934.

Comtemporary Communitarianism

Bellah, Robert. et al, *Habits of the Heart*, 1985.

Carson, Rachel. *Silent Spring*, 1962.

Daly, Herman, and John Cobb. *For the Common Good*, 1989.

McGregor, Douglas. *Human Side of Enterprise*, 1960.

Polanyi, Karl. *The Great Transformation*, 1944.

Postman, Neil. *Technopoly: The Surrender of Culture*, 1992.

Schumacher, E. F. *Small is Beautiful: Economics as if People Mattered*, 1973.

Tu Wei-ming, "A Confucian Perspective on the Rise of Industrial East Asia." *The American Academy of Arts And Sciences Bulletin* (October 1988).

Democracy

Basic Readings

Madison, James. Federalist Paper No. 10, 1787–88.

Mannheim, Karl. *Ideology and Utopia*, 1929.

Montesquieu, Charles de. *The Spirit of Laws*, 1748.

"The Progressive Party Platform of 1912." *The World Almanac, 1913*.

Roosevelt, Theodore. "The New Nationalism." In *The New Nationalism*, 1910.

Strachey, John. *The Challenge of Democracy*, 1963.

Toffler, Alvin. *The Third Wave*, 1980.

Contemporary Readings

Adler, Mortimer J. *Haves Without Have-Nots,* 1991.
Berlin, Isaiah. *The Crooked Timber of Humanity,* 1991.
Cleveland, Harlan. *Birth of A New World: An Open Moment for International Leadership,* 1993.
Dahl, Robert. *Democracy and Its Critics,* 1989.
De Pree, Max. *Leadership is an Art,* 1987.
Drucker, Peter. *The Unseen Revolution,* 1976.
Gardner, John. *Toward a Pluralistic but Coherent Society,* 1980.
Havel, Vaclav. *Summer Meditations,* 1992.

General Readings

Adler, Mortimer J. ed. *A Syntopicon of the Great Books of the Western World,* 1952.
Bell, Daniel. "The Cultural Wars: American Intellectual Life, 1965–1992. *Wilson Quarterly* (Summer 1992).
Heilbroner, Robert. *The Worldly Philosophers,* 1953.
Van Doren, Charles. *A History of Knowledge,* 1990.

Note: Most of the Basic Readings are used in either the Aspen Institute's Executive Seminar or in the Institute's Corporation and Society Seminar.

Acknowledgments

In the winter of 1973, I found myself a participant in Mortimer J. Adler's Aspen Executive Seminar. In our scheduled free time, the other seminar participants skied and enjoyed Aspen's fleshpots. Not me. I read and read, but didn't feel in the least deprived. It wasn't the case that I was habitually drawn to asceticism, but I was having the time of my life doing something that I had never really enjoyed before attending Mortimer's seminar. Although I had obtained degrees at two fine universities, I had never before been excited intellectually. But Mortimer set my previously underemployed brain cells to work and, as a consequence, I learned more in his two-week seminar than I had learned in seven years of formal higher education. I needed a framework to retain all the ideas I was absorbing in the seminar, and this motivated me to sketch the compass that provides the structure for this book.

That it took me two decades to put on paper what Mortimer taught in two weeks is, I trust, a tribute to the breadth and depth of his knowledge rather than an accurate indicator of my snail-like pace of working. In fact, in 1989, James Nelson, Executive Vice President of the Aspen Institute, provided the needed stimulus for me to finally write this book. He approached me with the idea of using the values compass as a discussion tool in a program conducted by the Institute for Information Studies (a joint venture of the Aspen Institute and the Northern Telecom corporation). Subsequently, David

McLaughlin, President of The Aspen Institute, and Michael Higgins, director of the Institute's seminar programs, generously invited me to spend the summer of 1991 in Aspen as a writer-in-residence, during which time I wrote the long-postponed first draft of this book.

Over the next few months, that rough manuscript benefitted greatly from Mortimer Adler's trenchant criticisms, from the editorial craftsmanship of Charles Van Doren, from Christopher Makins's delicate nudging on matters of substance and style, and from Walter Coyne's fine literary hand. Many useful contributions came from John Gardner, Judy Brown, Peter Brown, Peter Thigpen, Gus Tyler, Joel Rosenblatt, Richard Mason, and James W. Kuhn.

Warren Bennis, Betty Friedan, Keith Berwick, and Marilyn O'Toole provided timely encouragement and sound advice about choosing a publisher. In that regard, I consider myself blessed that the book found its way to Oxford University Press's skilled editors Herb Addison, Martha Ramsey, and Mary Sutherland. Finally, Susan Crissinger served ably as my proofreading maven.

I wish to thank each of these individuals for sharing time, ideas and resources. They are true friends and colleagues all.

Malibu, California   J. O'T.
March 1993

Name Index

160 *Name Index*

ish lexicographer and author),
69
Johnson, Lyndon (1908–1973;
U.S. president), 58

Kant, Immanuel (1724–1804; German philosopher), 39, 43, 108,
151
Kelso, Louis (1913–1991; U.S.
lawyer/economist), 116
Keynes, John Maynard (1883–
1946; British economist), 73,
85–86, 153
King, Martin Luther, Jr. (1929–
1969; U.S. civil rights leader),
20, 54, 152
Kobayashi, Yotaro (1933–   ;
Japanese business leader), 153
Kuan Yew, Lee (1923–   ;
Singapore prime minister), 75

Lapham, Lewis (1920–   ; U.S.
author), 120
Lenin, V. I. (1870–1924; Russian
revolutinary leader), 71–72
Lewis, Flora (1922?–   ; U.S.
journalist), 114–15
Lincoln, Abraham (1809–1865;
U.S. president), 5, 6, 54
Locke, John (1632–1704; British
philosopher), 19, 29, 36–39,
43, 45, 48–49, 57, 83–84, 90,
151–52

McGregor, Douglas (1906–1964;
U.S. management expert), 87,
154
Machiavelli, Niccolo (1469–1527;
Italian political philosopher and
statesman), 74, 153
Madison, James (1751–1836;
U.S. president), 37, 41, 51, 67,
109–110, 113, 115–16, 119,
154

Mann, Horace (1796–1859; U.S.
educational reformer), 51–52
Mannheim, Karl (1893–1947; German sociologist), 129–30, 154
Mao, Tse-tung (1893–1976; Chinese communist leader), 56,
89
Marshall, Alfred (1842–1924; British economist), 49, 72–73
Marx, Karl (1818–1883; German
philosopher), 13, 20, 29, 46,
48–51, 57, 63, 67, 71–72, 84–
90, 103, 106, 120, 152
Maslow, Abraham (1908–1970;
U.S. psychologist), 87
Mayhew, David (1937–   ; U.S.
political scientist), 114
Melville, Herman (1819–1891; U.S.
novelist), 152
Mill, Harriet Taylor (1807–1858;
British philosopher), 20, 46, 152
Mill, John Stuart (1806–1873; British philosopher), 20, 29, 38–
41, 43, 46, 49, 51, 57–58, 62,
67, 71, 88–89, 103, 108, 116,
151
Montesquieu, Charles-Louis
(1689–1755; French political
philosopher), 108, 119, 154
Morita, Akio (1921–   ; Japanese
industrialist), 74, 94

Niebuhr, Reinhold (1892–1971;
American philosopher), 107
Newton, Isaac (1632–1727; British
philosopher and mathematician), 79
Nye, Joseph (1937–   ; U.S. political scientist), 13

Okun, Arthur (1928–1980; U.S.
economist), 58–59, 62, 102, 153
Owen, Robert (1771–1858; British
industrialist), 29, 46, 87, 154